VISUAL NOTES
for Architects and Designers

VISUAL NOTES
for Architects and Designers

Norman Crowe
Associate Professor, School of Architecture
University of Notre Dame

Paul Laseau
Professor, Department of Architecture
Ball State University

JOHN WILEY & SONS, INC.

New York   Chichester   Weinheim   Brisbane   Singapore   Toronto

This text is printed on acid-free paper. ☉

Copyright © 1984 by Paul Laseau, Norman Crowe and John Wiley & Sons

Published simultaneously in Canada.

This publication is designed to provide accurate and authoritative information in regard to the subject matter covered. It is sold with the understanding that the publisher is not engaged in rendering legal, accounting, or other professional services. If legal advice or other expert assistance is required, the services of a competent professional person should be sought.

98   99   00   01   15   14   13   12

Library of Congress Cataloging-in-Publication Data

Crowe, Norman.
    Visual notes for architects and designers.
    Bibliography: p.
    Includes index.
    1. Communication in architectural design.   2. Visual
perception.   I. Laseau, Paul, 1937-   .   II. Title.
NA2750.C76   1983   720'.28   82-23786
ISBN 0-471-28959-0 (pbk.)

Preface

While this book was in preparation, *The Sketch Books of Le Corbusier* were published. These notebooks, written by a man who was to become the most influential architect of the twentieth century, are an effective example of what we intend to encourage. Their clear expression of enthusiasm, intense curiosity and probing, and incisive intelligence provide an inspiring example of that illuminating dialectic between thought and vision.

Le Corbusier's notes might be intimidating for some who are hesitant to compare themselves with an artist whose reputation sets him apart. But a close look at Le Corbusier's travel notes should dispel such awe. The drawings are not, in themselves, beautiful. They are notes, not intended to impress or entertain. They are sketchy, even scratchy; sometimes they overlap one another, some are crossed out and others are not easily deciphered because they are too crude to be articulate to anyone but the author. How could these drawings and scribbled notes be of any intrinsic value or practical use? A more careful inspection of these pages reveals that these verbal and visual notes are packed with thought. The drawings are not unsuccessful attempts to recreate visual reality but rather they are notes which record features which embody universal principles or simply useful observations. The visual notes are like verbal notes recorded from a lecture, speech, or book. They extract from the body of the whole that which can stand alone as an idea with a life of its own.

The purpose of *Visual Notes* is to encourage visual literacy. It is based upon the assumption that visual literacy should rank beside verbal literacy in importance. In an effort to encourage the development of a capability for communicating visual information, we have assembled examples which demonstrate how one can record visual information in much the same way that most verbal information is recorded. These examples show how taking visual notes is very much like taking notes generally except that the information being recorded is primarily in graphic rather than in verbal form.

We hope this book will awaken a realization that making notational drawings is both useful and easy. All too frequently we are dissuaded from drawing anything because we assume that it would be futile to do so unless we are endowed with the appropriate artistic talents. On the other hand, we are not discouraged from writing letters or taking notes in a lecture or drafting reports because we are not accomplished authors. We recognize the utility of writing and we forge ahead, undaunted by the obviously greater literary skills of others because we do not expect our work to be of exceptional literary quality. We only expect it to be clear and accurate, not necessarily beautiful. Had we this same attitude about visual communication, we could gain access to an equally intriguing and useful medium, one which complements our abilities in other areas and expands our knowledge of ourselves and the world around us.

This book is written so that anyone who wishes to gain access to the medium of notational drawing can do so by perusing the examples which we have provided and by "jumping in" without hesitation; that is, by beginning to do what the examples demonstate.

Because both of us are architects, we have leaned heavily upon examples from our own professional backgrounds. We assume that the examples from our field demonstrate general principles. Because most people are intimately familiar with towns and buildings through their own daily experience, towns and buildings as seen by architects provide examples which are as easy to become involved with as any. In addition, we have included examples from other areas of interest, such as music, literature, engineering, science, and travel. They are intended to demonstrate the broad range of application of visual notation for recording information, solving problems, and facilitating understanding.

Finally, we have written this book to satisfy a need which we have seen to be unanswered by other available sources. Students and practitioners in architecture and many other fields have a need to gather visual information. We have conducted students through field investigations and foreign study programs and have worked with other professionals in field investigations and have observed intrepid architects, botanists and others, struggling to understand a complicated set of conditions and to record their understanding for future reference. It is to this end that we have focused our attention in *Visual Notes*: the ability to record visual information which enhances and expands our knowledge, understanding, and effectiveness in a rich and complicated world.   NC/PL

ACKNOWLEDGMENTS

We want to thank Judith DiMaio, Richard Wesley and Jack Wyman for reading drafts of this manuscript and patiently giving us their advice. We are especially grateful to all the contributors to Chapter 4, whose drawings do so much to enhance the credibility of the premises for this book. Finally we thank the many others who were willing to discuss the topics of this book with us, providing new insights, information and inspiration as we assembled the ideas and images that made their way to these pages.

Contents

Introduction

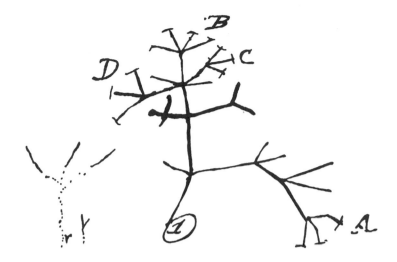

1-1 Charles Darwin's tree diagrams, representing traceable evolution in biological species.

Visual notes are simply the graphic equivalent of written notes. "Taking visual notes" refers to recording information which is primarily visual and, therefore, could not be recorded as effectively with words.

Keeping notes has always been an effective hedge against an imperfect memory. Moreover, the act of taking notes, selecting and sifting through them, is an important tool for creativity. Keeping a notebook of observations and experiences is a very old custom. Once visual notes were seen by architects to be nearly as important as verbal ones. Sketching was a common part of travel and education for the young architect.

Since the availability of easy, inexpensive photography, however, visual note-taking has declined. With this decline has come a decline in visual literacy in general. We have come to rely upon a camera to do all that notational sketches once did. Of course, a camera can do much of what sketching once did and it can perform certain tasks much faster and better. But a camera cannot record concepts, underlying structure, schematic organization, or anything else that the eye cannot see all at once. Although the camera *can* be used creatively, it does not *require* any more than a superficial level of interaction between the observer and the view. It can become a comparatively neutral instrument which neither demands a high degree of selectivity nor promotes out of necessity a very high level of understanding. Le Corbusier said that cameras "get in the way of seeing." Because visual notes do not accompany verbal ones as frequently as they once did, we believe that something valuable has been lost. It is our purpose to encourage the development and use of visual skills, especially in the form of simple, rapid, effective visual notation. We contend that the stigma against the use of graphic skills by those other than artists is based upon a false assumption that one must be an artist, heavily endowed with artistic aptitudes, in order to draw. Although a certain kind of drawing is the province of artists, that should not discourage others from using drawings to communicate information any more than one might refuse to ever write anything down because one is not an accomplished journalist or author. Making visual notes can be useful and effective and it can also be a particularly enjoyable endeavor. Once one has gotten beyond the notion that one's drawings have to be works of art, the activity of drawing gains a momentum of its own and inevitably provides a certain satisfaction of its own.

 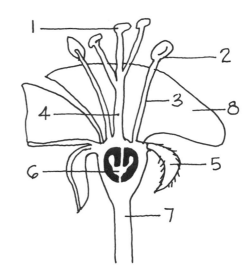

1-2

THE USES OF VISUAL NOTES

Who would have need for making visual notes? It might be: an engineer inspecting machinery, a scientist or laboratory technician recording a particular arrangement of apparatus, a landscape architect noting an exemplary design, an architect recording important details of a building which he intends to remodel or expand, a traveler wishing to record what lies beyond myriad impressions as he explores a new place, or a student simply taking notes during a slide lecture in biology, botany, anthropology, architectural or art history or other subject where visual form is a concern.

Visual notation has an additional important use. It records that which *cannot* be seen directly by the eye or by a camera. A laboratory technician draws a diagram of the assembly of various apparatus; it would not be useful for him to draw a picture of the laboratory. The architect's drawing demonstrates how the building he is studying is organized, a plan of how the circulation system works, or how and where the structural elements relate to the other parts of the building. A botanist draws an exploded view of a portion of a plant, showing how sustenance is carried through the veining to distant parts of the plant and how the flower's reproductive parts fit together. Visual notes record information which has been selected to be stored, studied, and communicated. Such drawings are often analytical; they take apart and describe rather than simply represent as in a picture. Compared to an artist's drawings, like a

sketch of a scene, visual notes require a lot of thought and comparably less skill because they are intended to disclose selective information, while the sketch of a scene requires little forethought but considerable skill to become an accurate depiction.

There is, however, still another important dimension to visual notation. We may be left with the impression that this form of graphic communication is only of concern to technologists and other professionals who require it for the conduct of their work, and that it is simply a useful, marketable skill. The effect, however, runs deeper. Consider an analogous situation: the effect of written language upon thoughts and actions. Not only does written language, with its commonly accepted vocabulary and grammar, communicate ideas, but it actually conditions the way we think. Moreover, it communicates our own thoughts, concepts, and ideas back to us. We use it to organize our thoughts as one does when one assembles what he has learned about a particular topic, records his thoughts and, finally, "gets it all down" in writing. It is in the act of "getting it all down" that new associations and understanding emerge as a result of giving order to what would otherwise be merely random thoughts and inert, factual circumstances. It is not surprising, therefore, that societies which had not developed a written language are not comparable with literate societies in terms of the quality of their accomplishments.

1-3 Arcade of the Villa Guilia in Rome, based on a drawing by Letarouilly.

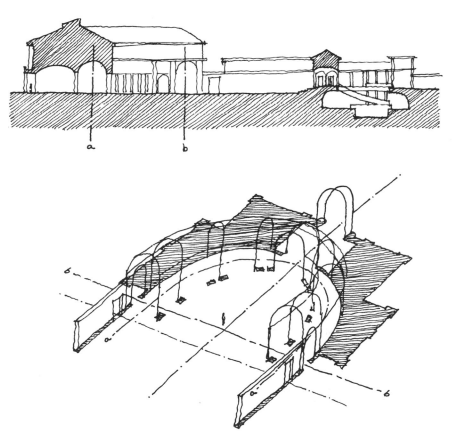

1-4 Visual notes of the same building, conveying a different kind of information than the pictorial drawing above.

1-5 Egyptian hieroglyphics: Words were formed by picture-symbols. Although a clumsy form of writing, the verbal and visual world were integrated in many early forms of writing.

Written language does have its limitations. Visual information is not as easily conveyed by the written word. Skillful writers have given us a special literary richness by describing something they wish us to see and feel, such as Balzac's description of the interior of an apartment on the Place des Vosges, or the Roman naturalist and writer Pliny's description of his villas in Italy in letters to his friends. But literature cannot convey all that seeing can provide. An amusing illustration is Durer's drawing of a walrus; it looks more like a hairless, wrinkled puppy with tusks! When Durer drew from life, his accuracy was unquestionable. But he had only briefly seen a walrus, and had only that fleeting memory and an elaborate verbal description from which to reconstruct an image of the animal.

It follows that just as verbal description is a source for a rich and profound level of understanding, visual literacy can provide its own access to a level of richness and understanding which would otherwise be unreachable. In our earlier description of the engineer, technician, scientist, and others making visual notes in order to facilitate their work, the impression might be that such notation is simply a means for the transfer of information. Certainly notes might serve only as information transfer and they might only be perceived as such. Although basic factual information is inert and without an intrinsic value, the very act of gathering the material, selecting, sorting, and "getting it down" can disclose new associations and promote a deeper understanding than any superficial observation could provide.

Communication, whether it is through literature, mathematics, music, or graphics, is at the very heart of creativity which thrives upon relationships drawn between symbols and ideas. The extent of one's creativity is related to the depth of one's experience of the world in which one lives. Imagination is built upon the richness of perceptions gleaned from an active and conscious participation in that world of thoughts and substance.

1-6 A lion drawn from life by Albrecht Durer.

1-7 A walrus drawn by Albrecht Durer. It is believed that this drawing was made from memory of a dead walrus he had seen.

1-8

VISUAL LITERACY

Verbal literacy is considered an essential skill in an industrialized, technologically-based society. Most of us have learned how to take verbal or written notes. We learn to understand others and express ourselves in a written language usually by the completion of high school. But understanding and expressing visual messages is a skill that remains poorly developed.

Visual literacy includes two skills: visual acuity and visual expression. Visual acuity is an intense ability to *see* information or multiple messages in one's environment with clarity and accuracy. When most people look at a house, they see a roof, windows, doors, or the colors of the walls. An artist also sees the lightness or darkness of the colors, the way the sun casts shadows, and the reflections in the windows. The architect also sees the types of materials used, the details of a window frame or eave, and the accessories such as gutters, downspouts and lights. The sociologist may see which windows have curtains drawn, what symbols are presented in the style of the

6

1-9

house, or how well the house is maintained. Visual expression is the ability to initiate visual messages. It is most strongly exhibited by people such as artists, designers, choreographers, photographers, or architects; but it is important to everyone. While visual acuity is concerned with the visual messages we receive, visual expression is concerned with the visual messages we send. Just as listening and speaking are related but distinct skills, seeing and expressing are interdependent but separate. Seeing is a necessary prelude to visual expression. But to achieve visual literacy both must be consciously developed. Since most readers will not start with these skills, they represent both a goal and a benefit of visual note-taking.

In *A Primer of Visual Literacy* D. A. Dondis has identified three levels of visual messages.[1] They are representation, abstraction, and symbolism. *Representation* seeks to accurately record what we can actually see or experience. Representative sketches function much as do photographs, but they are, of necessity, more selective. The photograph accurately duplicates all that can be seen from a specific vantage point; the representative sketch describes those parts of a view which are of special interest to the person sketching. While a photograph is a reproduction of what is visible, the sketch is a record of *how one sees* that which is visible. Producing sketches and "reading" other people's sketches provide both a view of the subject and an education about a variety of ways of seeing.

In visual communication, *abstraction* can be seen as a "simplification toward a more intense and distilled meaning."[2] We are literally bombarded with visual information at any given moment; in order to function in the world we must create some order and meaning out of what we see. This is basically the process of abstraction called perception. If we visit someone's house, the whole facade may be visible but we notice the front walk and front door because they are important to our intention to enter the house. While perception usually operates on a subconscious, reflex level, abstraction can be brought to a conscious, purposeful level when incorporated in a visual message. Abstractions may place emphasis on certain parts of a representational sketch such as the pattern of windows in a house; or they may be illustrations of that which cannot be seen such as the probable structural system of the house.

Symbolism is also a form of simplification of visual messages but it employs a surrogate or substitute image for what can actually be seen. In place of a representational drawing of a specific house we can use a symbol which most people accept as standing for the general concept "house." The advantage of using such a symbol is that it can be quickly drawn and miniaturized so that many symbols can be shown in the same space it takes to draw one house. These symbols can be arranged in an abstract "environment" in which the sequence, position, or grouping of the symbols conveys additional information.

A variety of examples of representational, abstract, and symbolic drawings can be found in other books. A partial list of sources is included in the bibliography for this book; and specific examples of drawing techniques are included in chapter 5.

1-10A Representative sketches.

1-11A Abstract sketches.

1-12A Symbolic sketches.

1-10B

1-10C

1-11B

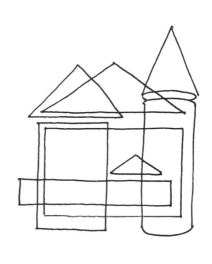

1-11C

1-12B

1-12C

1-13

THE NOTEBOOK

In keeping a notebook we use combinations of representational, abstract, and symbolic messages. This requires our understanding of the basic approach to creating each type of drawing and the ways in which they can be combined. When children draw a person, they draw symbols for all the parts they know must be there to make a human figure. The head is a circle and the body a larger circle below the head. Eyes are represented by two dots; nose, mouth, and hair by appropriately placed lines; arms and legs by single lines emanating from the body circle. Likewise, a house is depicted as a rectangle with a triangle on top of it and a symbolic window with a single crossed division on it resides on the facade. Our training in school in mathematics and written language reinforces our tendency toward symbolic drawings.

In her book, *Drawing on the Right Side of the Brain,* Dr. Edwards describes the transition from symbolic drawings to producing nonsymbolic drawings as a process of limiting the involvement of the portion of our brain which deals primarily with verbal information. Then that portion of our brain which processes visual information can take over. Rather than the drawing being comprised of symbolic elements, it becomes a composition of shapes which represent the visual likeness of that which we are recording.

If one wishes to produce a true likeness, like an accurate photograph of something, it is important to draw the shape accurately, just as it is seen, and not to permit preconceived form or symbolic gestures to intercede. Dr. Edwards describes this as "locking out the left side of the brain" and

10

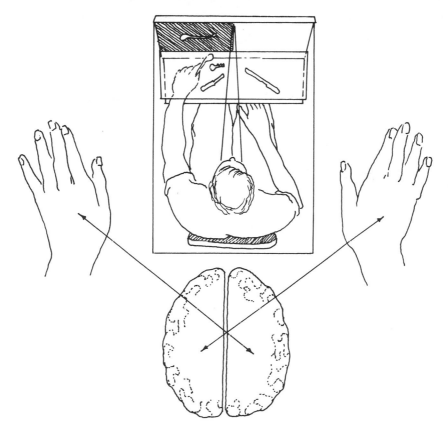

1-14 Based on a drawing by Betty Edwards. Research reveals that the two sides of the brain function in relative independence, with different functional "assignments" which, on occasion, can conflict with one another.

she proposes exercises intended to facilitate this locking-out process. Later in this book, we describe her technique in greater detail and we propose some exercises in response to some of the discoveries her book discusses. Among the exercises she proposes is one whereby you reproduce a drawing upside down. The drawing which you are to reproduce is, preferably, one which is unintelligibile to you until it is finally righted; you are therefore forced to draw the form as it is seen, without regard to what is actually depicted in the original drawing. The lines, proportions, and tones are seen and copied simply as lines, proportions, and tones and nothing more. This keeps the verbal part of our brain from dominating these processes and short-circuiting them with symbolic elements and memories of simplified versions of the subject being drawn.

Lyman Evans
April 2, 1978

Lyman Evans
May 8, 1978

Gerardo Campos
September 2, 1973

Gerardo Campos
November 10, 1973

1-15 These pairs of drawings were made at the beginning and the end of a drawing course which stressed techniques for "locking out" left brain dominance. The beginning drawings rely upon symbolic representation of parts of the face, as do childrens' drawings, while the end drawings reproduce visual form.

Visual notation is not always the same as the realistic drawing mode described above, but it shares certain characteristics with lifelike drawing skills such as those Dr. Edwards' techniques seek to teach. As you will see in the ensuing examples, an accurate representation of shape and proportion is frequently important, even though reproduction of optical accuracy is not always the goal in visual notation. In optically accurate drawings, lines are drawn onto a flat piece of paper as an abstraction of the depicted object or scene. Seen in light of a child's propensity to draw symbolic objects rather than the actual subject being depicted we assert the importance of recognizing optical qualities of perspective and visual recognition of form, shape, and proportion. Visual notation will not necessarily depict objects as seen, but rather they might be shown from above or below, with portions removed or rotated to show what cannot be seen in a single view. The shape and proportions of the object must still be reasonably accurate with respect to the unrealistic view; therefore some basic drawing skills are a prerequisite to making visual notes. Basic drawing skills arise out of the note-taking process. The sketchy approach to visual note-taking and especially the speed which is thereby induced, tends to take care of problems of accurate depiction as you progress. If, after several attempts at visual note-taking, you cannot grasp the means for recording shape and proportion with reasonable accuracy, we suggest that you refer to chapter 5 or you might spend some time with Dr. Edwards' book. Then you may return to your visual notebook, having gained more confidence in your ability to make your pen or pencil record shape and proportion with acceptable accuracy.

1-16 Albrecht Durer's illustration of perspective theory based upon sight lines and a "picture plane".

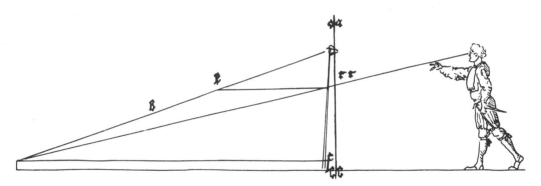

1-17 Based on an illustration by Albrecht Durer explaining the mechanics of optical perspective.

1-18 A scene in Venice by the architect, Louis I. Kahn, recorded in his notebook when he was a young man.

USING THIS BOOK

This book consists largely of examples of the use of visual notes. They have been arranged in order of relative complexity and present issues which tend to build upon one another. However, these examples need not be studied in the order in which they are presented. This book can be seen as a reference source, permitting the reader to thumb through to find an example which parallels a problem at hand. The examples demonstrate techniques for recording visual information, varying from one another in style, graphic skill, complexity or simplicity of technique. We have provided a potpourri of examples so that there will be something for many needs, interests, and levels of skill. Furthermore, certain examples which might convey very little to the reader at first, might be seen in a different light as needs, skills, and interests develop.

Chapter 2 describes the basic processes of note-taking. Then chapter 3 provides an idea of the effect of accumulated visual notes in the form of a journal. In chapter 4 we have collected examples of visual notes from several people representing a wide range of skills, style, and subjects; we hope by this means to stretch your recognition of the potential of visual notation. Finally, chapter 5 presents several practical suggestions for keeping a visual notebook.

GETTING STARTED

Children are typically uninhibited about drawings. They are unconcerned as to whether their drawings look professional or not, or whether someone else understands them. Their drawings are spontaneous expressions of a less inhibited spirit. Children will often throw a completed drawing aside or give it away to make room for beginning another. Their drawings are not seen by them as precious objects; it is the act of making them to which they are attracted rather than the production of objects for later contemplation, use or enjoyment.

A child's frame of mind concerning drawing is enviable because he proceeds without hesitation. Sometimes artists and drawing teachers encourage their students to return to that childhood innocence in order to get them over that initial reluctance to "mess up a clean sheet of paper." We, too, would

encourage the reader to jump into the process of drawing, setting aside any expectation of artful graphics.

Finally, to get going find a sketch pad or notebook that you can keep with you most of the time and start using it. If you are not yet skillful enough to work at the level of complexity you wish, we suggest that you combine photocopies and traced sheets with drawn information in your notebook. A photocopy can be traced with various color pencils or it can be overlaid with a transparent sheet to produce a composite image. It is important to get started by whatever means or motivation is available to you. As in writing, one becomes more skilled at visual note-taking as one uses this approach to gathering information and you will become more aware of its potential usefulness as skill and familiarity increase.

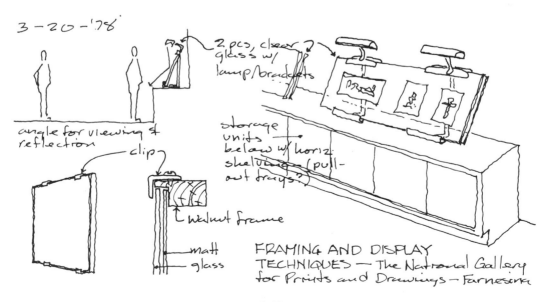

3-20-'78

2 pcs, clear ? glass w/ lamp/brackets

angle for viewing & reflection

clip

storage units below w/ horiz shelving (pull-out trays?)

walnut frame

matt glass

FRAMING AND DISPLAY TECHNIQUES — The National Gallery for Prints and Drawings — Farnesina

1-19

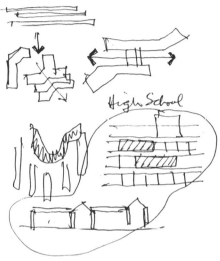

2-1

This book contains examples of visual notes taken by a variety of people in a variety of contexts. This chapter provides a "guidebook" to the experiences of visual note-taking. Like all guidebooks, this one is not a substitute for direct experience, but it can sharpen perceptions and heighten the intensity of your exposure to visual notes. You should note that the examples in this chapter are formally presented, as are many in this book, for the sake of clarity. As you begin your note-taking, your drawings may not and need not be this precise to still be effective for you.

The creative process requires three activities: gathering information about the various factors in a design problem (requirements, contexts, forms); analysis of the information to gain an understanding of the design problem (relationships, hierarchy of needs, generic solutions); devising of specific solutions to the design problem (concepts, construction, expression). Each of the activities—recording, analysis, and design—are contexts within which visual note-taking can be of great help to the designer.

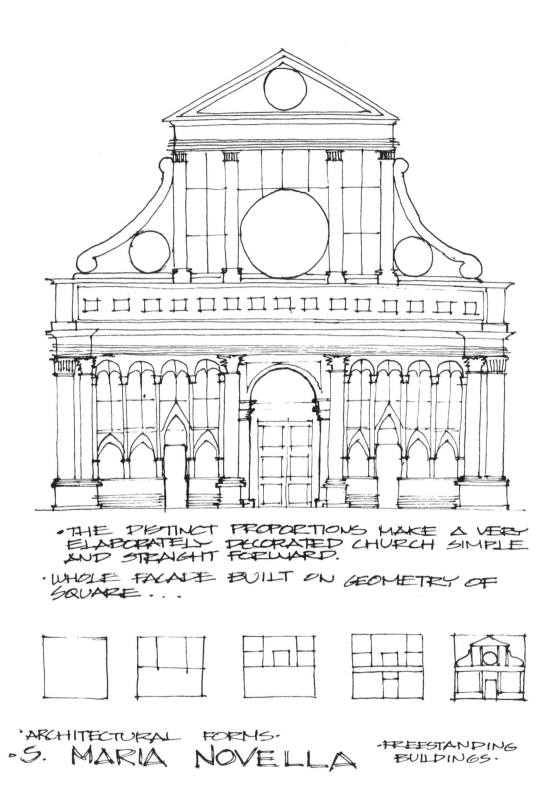

- THE DISTINCT PROPORTIONS MAKE A VERY ELABORATELY DECORATED CHURCH SIMPLE AND STRAIGHT FORWARD.
- WHOLE FACADE BUILT ON GEOMETRY OF SQUARE...

ARCHITECTURAL FORMS.
- S. MARIA NOVELLA   - FREESTANDING BUILDINGS.

2-2 Facade studies of Santa Maria Novella by Douglas Garofalo.

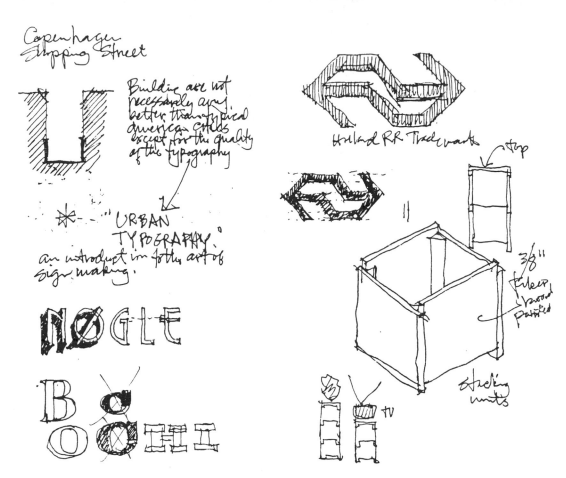

2-3 Notebook entries.

RECORDING

The foundation of design and, therefore, of note-taking, is the collection of information. Designing is difficult without practice at analyzing problems, developing solutions, and testing those solutions; but designing is impossible without information about the specific problem, design precedents, and the world in which we live. While it is true that the quality of our design process improves through practice, it is also true that the quality of the results, our designs, depends upon the quality and variety of our experience of environment and life.

Many people may witness the same environment or event but no two of them will have the same experience. Some people, including designers, go through their lives deriving little experience from what they have seen; their attention to their environment remains at one level. A successful

designer depends upon experiences and, therefore, is concerned with the way in which he or she gains those experiences. Architects and designers have turned to daily note-taking as a means of recording experiences and, equally important, of developing visual acuity which will improve the intensity of their experiences. Many architects start note-taking while traveling as a way to record direct impressions of a new environment, but there are many other opportunities for note-taking including lectures, seminars, workshops, visiting a store, reading a book, or viewing television. Recording information in each of these situations requires a combination of skills: observation, perception, discrimination, and communication. To get a good start at visual note-taking we need to understand each of these skills.

2-4 Stereotypical.

2-5 Representative.

Observation

It seems obvious that in order to draw something one needs first to look at it, but the difficulty that most people have with drawing is a result of not taking the time to look carefully. Betty Edwards has described how it is that most people fail to observe what they attempt to draw.[3] Most of our thinking is dominated by the left side of the brain which is adept at symbolizing, abstracting, and rationalizing while the functions of the right side of the brain, spatial perception, detail observation, and pattern recognition, are suppressed. The left side of the brain is easily frustrated and fatigued by attempts at careful observation and therefore continually pushes us away from observation toward the use of sym-

bols, cliche, or easy convention. A typical example of this left brain dominance is the common use of stereotype features when drawing human faces. Not only do these faces appear unrealistic, but in drawing them we have learned nothing about faces in general or these faces in particular; we have not *looked* at the faces we are supposed to be drawing. Left brain dominance is not reserved for the novice; it is a constant force which can even affect people with some training in drawing; when architectural students are left on a street corner to draw the buildings they see, many of them will draw an aerial perspective, a view which could be had only by a fifty-foot tall observer.

2-6 Stereotypical.

2-7 Representative.

2-8

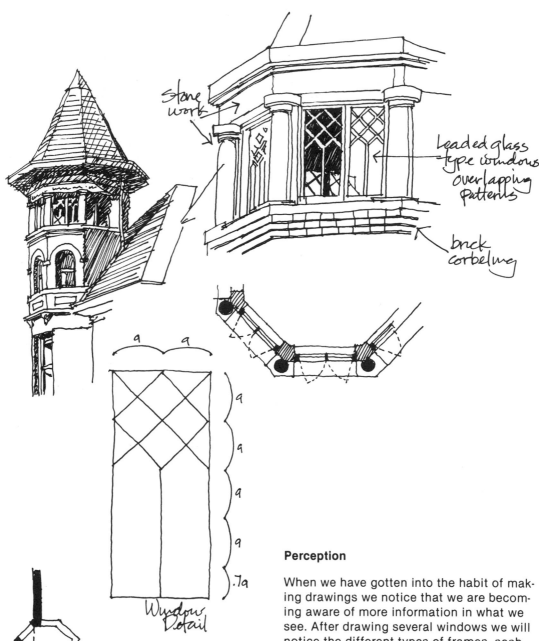

stone
work

Leaded glass
type windows
overlapping
patterns

brick
corbeling

9   9

9

9

9

9

.7a

Window
Detail

Engagement of
Octagon

2-9 Residence-Evansville, Indiana.

Perception

When we have gotten into the habit of making drawings we notice that we are becoming aware of more information in what we see. After drawing several windows we will notice the different types of frames, sash and mullions, the reflections in the glass, and the shapes of curtains or blinds behind the glass. This information is not just a means to make a more realistic sketch but important information about the nature of form and its contribution to experience. Because the purpose of a notebook is communication rather than producing pretty drawings, there are many options for recording these new perceptions: we can add written notes with arrows to call out information; a larger scale sketch of a particular item can be used to obtain a more detailed and accurate record; the original sketch can be supplemented with plan and section views or diagrams to include many more observations.

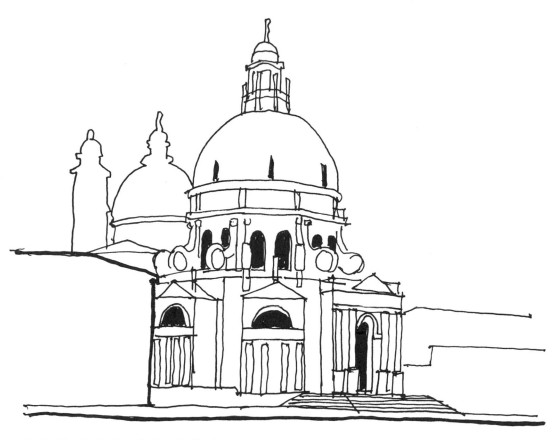

2-10 Santa Maria della Salute, Venice.

Discrimination

The complement to increased perception is discimination. Although we can expect to improve the speed and accuracy with which we take visual notes, time is a constraint for even the most accomplished drawer. While being aware of many levels of information, we may wish to concentrate on specific information of special importance to our work; in so doing we exercise discrimination concerning the topics of our notes. Discrimination may also be made concerning the type of notation; some designers achieve significant efficiencies in their notes through the use of abstractions which make the drawings useful to themselves even if not easily understood by others. Particularly good models in this respect are the drawings by cartoonists; it is the nature of their form of communication to strive for utmost economy of means. Their drawings exhibit a simplicity, clarity, and impact worth study.

COMMUNICATION VARIABLES:

MESSAGE
RECEIVER
MEDIA
LOCATION
TIME
SEQUENCE
ENVIRONMENT
OBJECTIVES

2-11 Bologna, Italy.

Communication

This last skill recognizes the end purpose of collecting information, namely to communicate with ourselves. Effective human communication must consider the intended receiver or audience, the communication media, and the context(s) for communication. Although these factors may vary from person to person, there are some general observations which may be helpful.

In planning for inner-personal communication, we have a significant advantage in that we have intimate knowledge of the receiver, ourself. Consider your habits of thinking, how you will use the recorded information, and the types of visual stimulus to which you respond. Some people do their most effective thinking when they can remove the clutter of information and concentrate on one idea at a time; others are stimulated by variety and ambiguity and enjoy searching for ideas amidst the clutter. There will be a difference in the form of information to which these two types of persons will best respond.

There are also differences in how the recorded information will be used; it may be used to construct an accurate model or perspective drawing of a three-dimensional space, as a basis for illustrating a design problem, or as a stimulus to further thinking about a specific subject. Each of these uses can be facilitated by a distinct type of visual message. Finally, the context for communication can vary greatly among persons, because it is made up of several factors: time, location, circumstances, environment, sequence, predisposition. For example, suppose your best opportunity to review your notes and think usually is during a plane or train ride. You may adjust for this by making simple, bold notes in a small notebook that can be carried in your pocket; and you may also leave white space on each page or at the back of the book for direct insertion of your future ideas. However, if you will normally be using your notebook in the studio where there is lots of room and time, the notes might be kept in a larger book with room for many notes on one page.

Pale blue
Beige
Darkest
obstructed view
Juxtaposition of scale
Plays of light

2-12 Charleston, South Carolina.

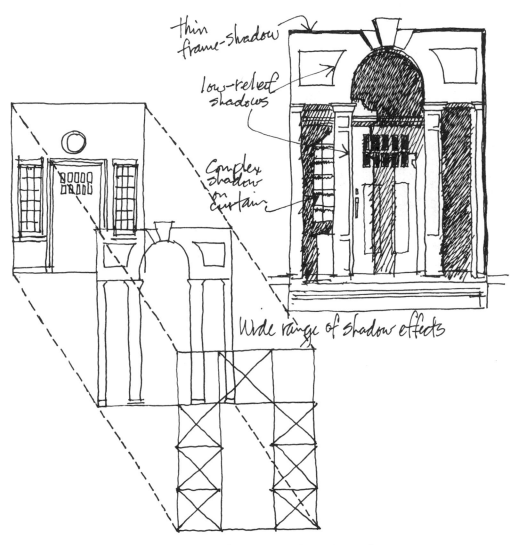

Handwritten annotations on drawing:
- thin frame-shadow
- low-relief shadows
- Complex shadow on curtain
- Wide range of shadow effects

2-13 Entry studies of a residence-Evansville, Indiana.

ANALYSIS

The second context for visual notation for the designer is the study of information previously gathered. As we have seen, the recording of information, in itself, can be a significant help to the architect or designer, but the potential of note-taking extends beyond recording. Powers of perception can grow through reflection as well as observation. Often a second look at a subject brings fresh insights or reveals new meanings. In order to get you started with this application of note-taking we will review skills useful to analysis: examination, abstraction, and restructuring.

Examination

The analysis of drawings can be a process of discovery just as it is in direct observation and much of the same advice is ap-

plicable (see OBSERVATION). We must not assume that because we took the notes that we are aware of all the information they contain; one of the values of good representative drawings is that there is often a subconscious reaction to the subject which finds its way into the drawings. A pattern of shadows may have originally been drawn because of its visual stimulation; upon re-examination, the designer is able to discover the source of the shadows. In another example, an original drawing includes multiple fluid lines, tentatively exploring a form; under study, these lines might suggest the inclusion of natural vegetation or curvilinear forms in the building being studied. These examinations can be noted with the use of new sketches or by the modification or enhancement of the original drawings.

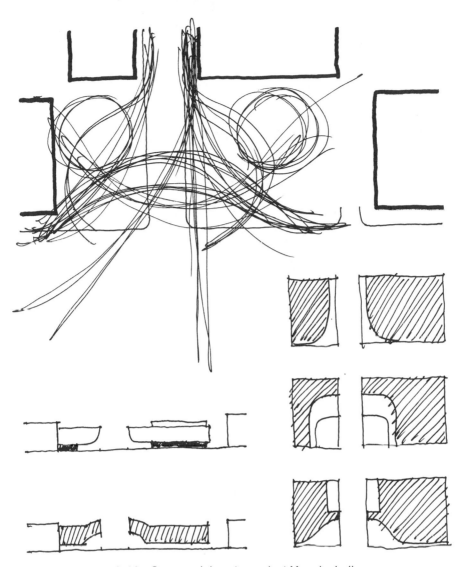

2-14 Commercial center project-Muncie, Indiana.

2-15 Courthouse-Santa Barbara, California.

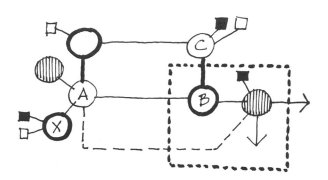

2-16 Bubble diagram.

Abstraction

Often analysis can be facilitated through the deliberate modification of the visual notes. One way to go about abstraction is to select only one or a few features for illustration; by drawing a simple outline of a building and the windows (in a contrasting tone) it is possible to see more clearly the pattern and relationships of the windows and their impact on the composition of the major building forms; drawing the reverse image of an urban complex in plan view may clarify the interaction between public and private space. Another form of abstraction is the conversion of visual notes to less specific forms, a type of visual code or language; this process can reveal generalizations and structures that are transferable to other contexts or design problems. The encoded image helps us to look past the particular style of a design to the composition of forms; it may also suggest additional meanings or functions of the design.

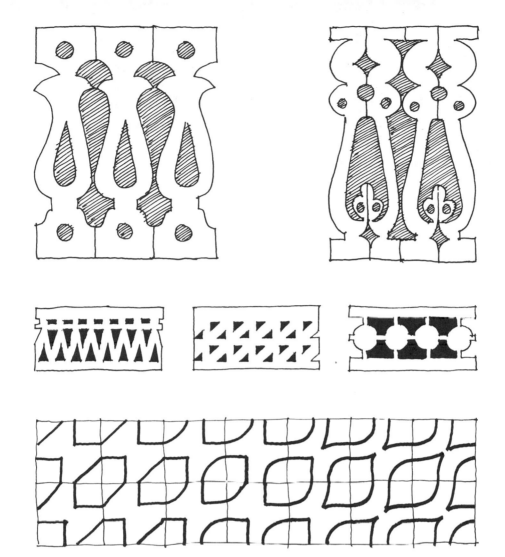

2-17 Pattern studies.

Restructuring

Frequently, analysis of visual notes leads to speculation about alternatives to the patterns that are being discovered. If boards in a railing have been cut to produce an interesting embellishment, it is instructive to explore the effect of different cuts in the boards. Also, there is a wide range of visual images which can result from the restructuring of abstracted drawings. These manipulations begin to move thinking and, therefore, note-taking into the other major context for designers: design studies.

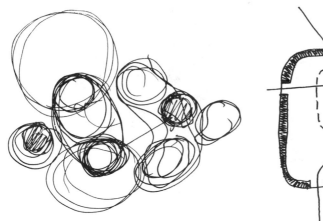

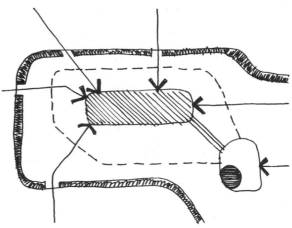

2-18 Relationships diagram.

2-19 Circulation diagram.

DESIGN

Many successful designers do not depend on commissions as their sole opportunity for designing or creativity; they are continually thinking about general design problems and inventing new forms. It is comparable to the practice of football teams between the big games. To be good at something like designing you must keep mentally in shape. A notebook can be a handy tool for this type of exercise and having a record of your experiences, analysis, and ideas in one place provides ready "food" for thought.

Encoding

Designers, especially architectural designers, consider a wide range of variables in producing designs, including human behavior, construction technology, and spatial definition. To help deal with all this information designers often encode it in a visual language which is highly symbolic and abstract; a few lines on paper may represent an entire building or the circulation needs for a community. As you work with note-taking you will be able to develop your own visual shorthand. Some suggestions for a visual notation system are included in chapter 5.

Flexible Thinking

A few years ago, James Adams wrote a very useful book entitled *Conceptual Blockbusting* in which he pointed out that often our creativity is hampered by mental blocks.[4] Habit or training in just one mode of thinking can cause us to ignore the many other ways to look at a problem. To take full advantage of our mind we need to be aware of the alternative ways of thinking and the techniques for shifting perceptions.

Note-taking can be an aid to flexible thinking by providing visual clues or triggers that shift perception and open new avenues of investigation. One example of this is the recasting of a plan drawing in an artificial geometric pattern; new relationships between parts are revealed and the truly unique functions may emerge. At the other extreme, a very loosely drawn plan view may uncover several alternative themes for the expression of spatial enclosure. Each of these insights should be pursued and their implications illustrated in order to take advantage of the shifts in thinking. Because the notebook is a permanent record, it is possible to pick it up at a future date and continue with ideas presently initiated.

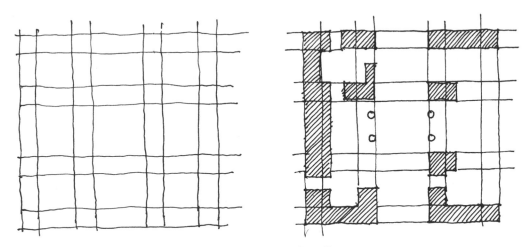

2-20 Use of geometric pattern.

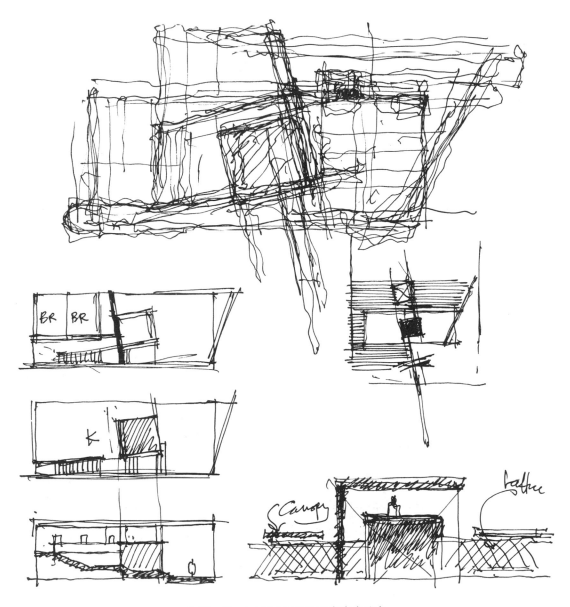

2-21 The loose or open-ended sketch.

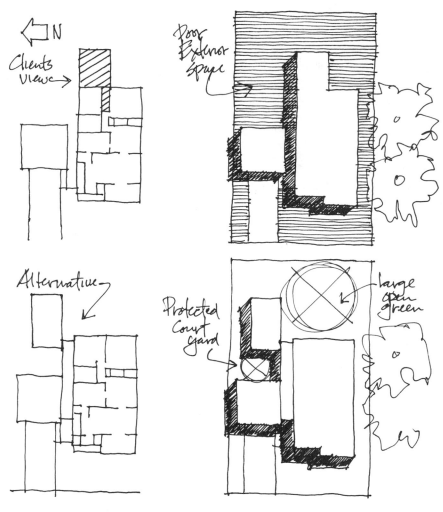

2-22 Site studies.

Opportunity Seeking

If design were simply a matter of solving problems, much of design activity could be eliminated and along with it would go much of the value of design. David Pye has brilliantly debunked the notion of "purely functional" design. He illustrates the presence of the human touch in all design including that which is supposed to be very objective such as structural design.[5] We also observe that design problems are not static; they change with time and are changed by the way we perceive them: a client may come to an architect with the problem of adding a room to the back of his house but the architect may expand the client's understanding of the problem to include energy consumption in the entire house or the impact of an addition upon the use of backyard space. The designer looks for opportunities while working with problems; he seeks not only the application of known solutions but the invention of new solutions which extend human experience and delight. One of the keys to inventing is the ability to see analogies between design problems and design solutions. Some time ago, Piet Hein, the

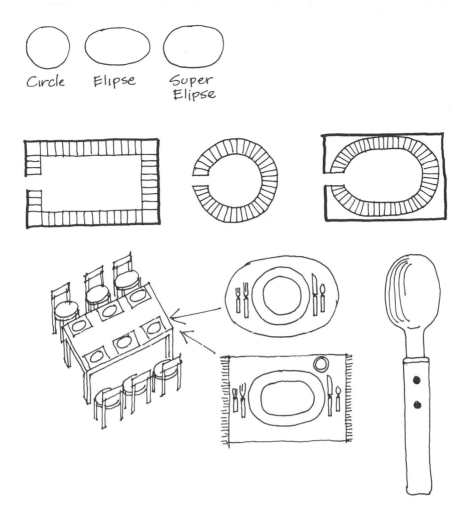

2-23 Shared solutions to analogous problems.

Danish mathematician and artist, was presented with the problem of fitting a circular parking arrangement within a rectangular space.[6] He devised a way of changing the formula of the ellipse to produce a fat or "super" ellipse as a compromise between the two shapes. Subsequently, he discovered many analogous problems to which this solution could be applied, including the fit between the roundness of dinner plates and the rectangular zones on the table on which they are placed. The illustration of problems and solutions in a notebook im-

proves your chances of seeing analogies, enhancing your thinking and designing. There are many other techniques for enhancing creativity, which can be applied through note-taking (see chapter 5). These can be added to your notebooks as you gain more experience.

With the capacities of visual notation for representation, abstraction, and symbolism in mind and an appreciation of their utility for the designer, we can now explore a specific notebook.

A Journal

3-1 The Acropolis in Athens, drawn by Charles Jeanneret (Le Corbusier) during his travels as a youth. SPADM, Paris/VAGA, New York 1982.

One's first motivation to make visual notes is likely to come from a very practical circumstance. Such notes are likely to be an extension of usual verbal note-taking occasions, such as students at lectures, or participants in a business meeting or a reader extracting essential elements from a book, an article, or a report. Once it becomes as easy to record visual thoughts as verbal ones, not only is an effective new access to practical information gained, but a new world of remarkable richness is opened as well. Beyond recording specific information for a particular and rather narrow purpose, lies the possibility of keeping a journal.

Keeping a journal is an old custom. We distinguish at this point between a notebook and a journal. The difference is mostly one of attitude and intention. A notebook is used to record notes in response to specific tasks such as remembering the significant points made in a lecture or book or gathering information in order to solve a particular problem in the course of one's occupation or avocation. A journal's function is to gather thoughts and images as they might arise, without regard to immediate priorities or assigned tasks. The word "journal" comes from the Latin word for "day," reflecting the intention of recording thoughts, experiences, and images on a daily basis. One need not think of a journal, however, as requiring daily feeding for its sustenance, but the implica-

tion is nonetheless that it is a long-term venture.

As the journal stretches over time, as over a journey or over several years, it becomes a record of a portion of its author's life. Looking back over a journal provides a journey back over events which might otherwise have been largely forgotten. Although a journal may be seen as an instrument for nostalgic reminiscences, it can do much more. It can serve to bring together thoughts and images which would otherwise be separated from one another by time, thereby preventing them from building upon one another as they might if seen in closer proximity. The writer Edward Fischer summed it up very well in an article which encouraged his readers to keep a journal: "Judged by the days, life does not make sense. Judged by the years, things add up and a plan emerges. A good reason to keep a journal is to have the consolation of seeing patterns form."[7]

As a journal grows it becomes something more than a record. Again according to Edward Fischer, it "encourages shaping those blurred notions and hunches into ideas you may be willing to stand behind. It helps you turn your inner chaos into something of a cosmos." The "cosmos" he spoke of is a personal one on one hand and an objective one on the other. Objective observations and personal responses are set down for reconsideration at another time. Fischer was referring to a written journal, but it follows that a journal which contains both written and visual works can be even more vital. The cosmos such a journal helps to build and serves to explore is composed both of thoughts, and of the images which generate them. According to G. K. Chesterton: "There is at the back of every artist's mind something like a pattern or a type of architecture. The original quality in any man of imagination is imagery. It is a thing like the landscape of his dreams; the sort of world he would like to make or in which he would wish to wander; the strange flora and fauna of his own secret planet; the sort of thing he likes to think about. This general atmosphere, the pattern or structure of growth, governs all his creations, however varied."[8]

In this chapter we have selected and reassembled pages from a journal. In doing so, we hope to convey the flavor as well as the utility of keeping a journal. As the journal progresses, discoveries are made, incidences that are separated by time and place are brought together, and patterns begin to emerge. The importance of this particular journal does not lie in the subjects it records but rather in the way they have been recorded and in the relationships which arise from their having been brought together. We have edited out pages so that the journal will not tire a reader with superfluity. In this respect, this journal is not an entirely realistic one. It is an assembly of related and nearly related observations brought together more closely than they would otherwise be so that we can demonstrate how a journal works and we can indicate what a journal can accomplish.

A discussion of literature or theater, for instance, must consider the content as well as the form of what is being considered. In this discussion of a journal we, likewise, discuss *what is being recorded* as well as *how it is recorded* because these two qualities are impossible to separate from one another. Therefore, there arises a sort of story-within-a-story as the journal progresses. On one hand there is our primary concern for demonstrating techniques for recording information and for showing how various bits of information interact, and on the other is the importance of understanding the information and thoughts that are being recorded so that technique and interaction can be understood. The notes consist of detailed investigations which were the result of specific assignments and of fragments of journeys and happenstance discoveries. Specific assignments result in what we term "case studies"; they cover a whole subject with some degree of thoroughness. The fragments and happenstance notes arrest what would otherwise have been fleeting images. In this way, by combining purposeful working notes in the form of case studies, with fragmentary thoughts in a journal we hope to suggest the breadth and potential inherent in visual notation. The best way to understand a journal is to proceed through it one page at a time along a concatenation of events and discoveries. Since each "episode" is an involved and rather complex event, they are best understood by "getting into them" along with the author. In so doing, you will share the enjoyment of discovery. You should consider this chapter as a story, told by the one who experienced it, to recount those experiences and to show what those experiences and observations lead to.

3-2

3-3

9-18-77 to 7-5-82

JOURNAL

Farm Complexes / Brittany and Normandy —————— Sept. 18, '77
Courtyards / Tuscany ————————————————————— Oct. 1, '77
Castelvecchio / Verona ——————————————————— Oct. 17, '77
American Academy lecture (R. Arnheim) / Rome ——— Feb. 3, '78
The Certosa / Pavia ————————————————————— Feb 5, '78
Truli and the olive groves / Alberobello —————— Mar. 6, 7, '78
Case del Fascio / Como ——————————————————— Mar 16, '78
Tobacco Company offices / Rome ———————————— Apr. 10, '78
Windows / Lund ——————————————————————— June 2, '78
Stockholm city plan / on flight from Helsinki ———— June 14, '78
Row houses / Phidelphia ——————————————————— June 16, '78
Midwest farm buildings / Southern Iowa —————— May 17, '79
Midwest Vernacular farm house - dtls. / Iowa, Ill. —— Aug 19, '79
Place des Vosges / Paris ——————————————————— May 11, 12, '81
Traditional Mediterranean windows / Rome ———— June 2, '81
Study of town organization / Urbino ——————— June 10, -13 '81
Thomas Jefferson's Quad / Univ. of Virginia ——— June 21, '81

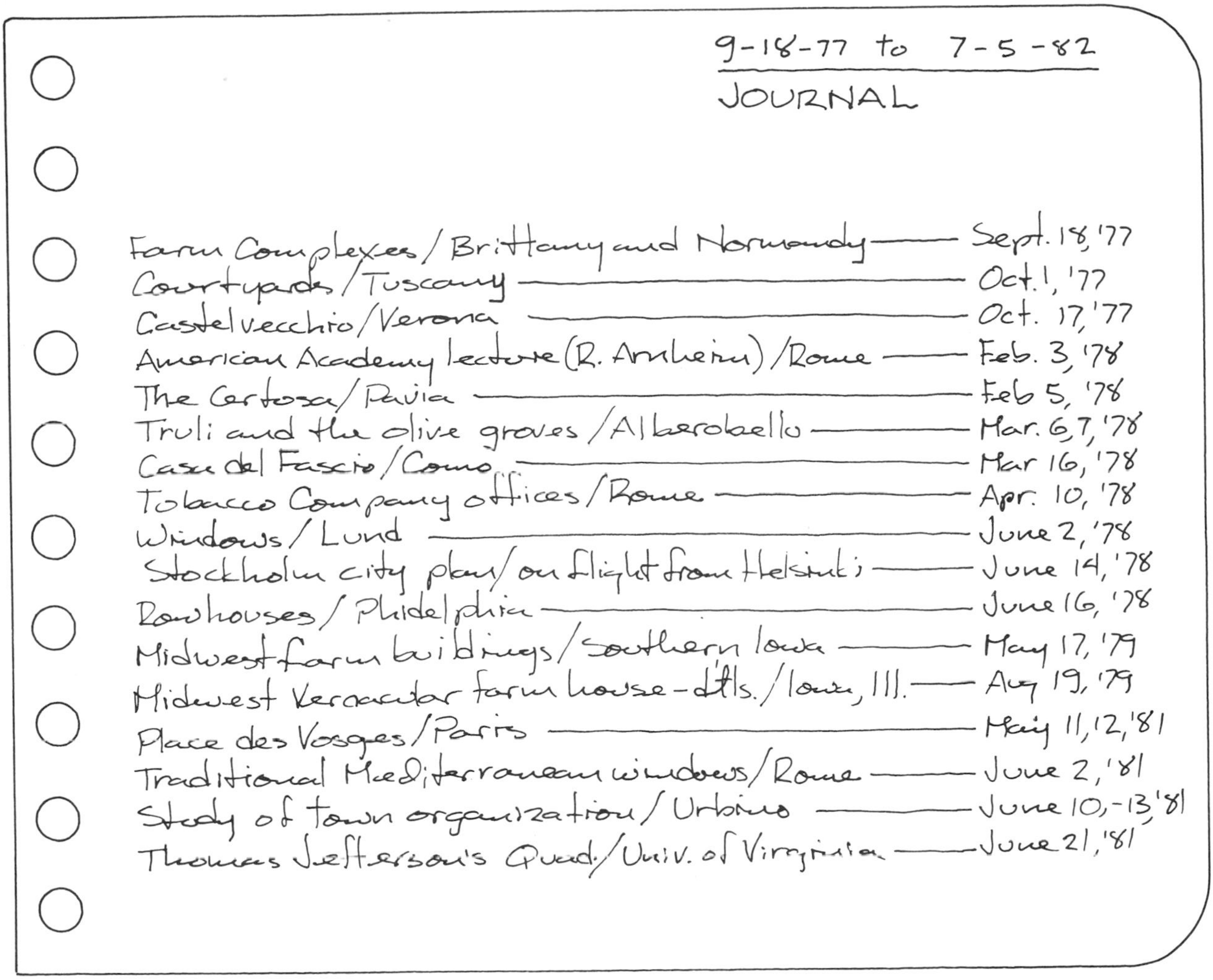

3-2 View of the Propylaea by Charles Jeanneret (Le Corbusier). A journal places scattered events in perspective, to help turn "chaos into something of a cosmos." SPADM, Paris/VAGA, New York 1982.

3-6-78

Alberobello

The ancient Romans had a term for it, *genius loci,* or sense of place. Apparently it was a very comprehensive concept, having to do with all the qualities of a place which, in combination, make it unique and special. The term could apply to a city or a region, or something so small as a grove of trees or the rooms and courtyards of a building. The architect and theorist, Christian Norberg-Schulz, maintains that this is a concept which remains as important to be aware of today as it was in Roman times.[9] For a designer, the sense of place is particularly important. Unless we understand the various qualities which come together to provide the essence of a place, we cannot modify that place without risking the destruction of its valuable characteristics.

Photographs or accurate drawings of a place, a small town for instance, would depict certain aspects that are important to the experience of it, but experience is much more elaborate than simply seeing something from several fixed points of view as pictures must do. Of course, no medium or combination of media can substitute for experiencing the place first hand. But words, pictures, and visual notes together can convey much of that which contributes to an overall character. Effective visual notes, words, and photographs can be particularly informative for subsequent design work which is either of a similar nature or which involves modifications to that place itself.

10 - 1 - 77

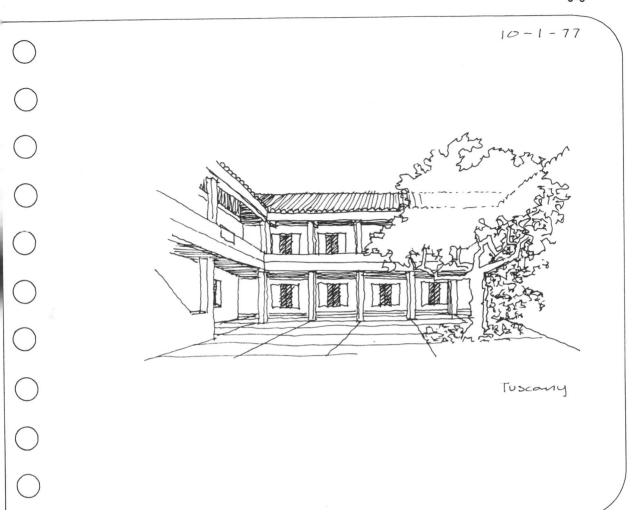

Tuscany

The following case studies and notes are concerned with the total unique identity of interesting places and experiences and with the characteristic details of which they are composed. The notes do not substitute for the experiences, but they convey essential characteristics which, when coupled with comparable experiences in the reader's own background, reproduce something of the flavor of the real thing. Most importantly the process of compiling these notes required a thorough and especially thoughtful effort by the person who wrote and drew them, thereby inducing a deeper understanding of what was being seen than would ever have resulted from a relatively passive "tourist" visit. The act of making these notes required a close look at fundamental relationships, as each successive effort led to another discovery which, in turn uncovered more questions about the nature of the place.

We have included a photograph of places being investigated so that the reader can compare the drawings with pictorial reality, and to provide a more comprehensive understanding of the essential characteristics of the place. The written notes are rather brief, owing to the knowledge of the writer and his reliance upon other sources of information such as books, maps, and brochures.

3-7

Our first case study is of a small Italian hill town which is said to be "in perfect balance." Urbino's population, economy, history, and its relationship with the hinterland are thought by many to constitute a perfect ratio with one another, thereby making it a place worthy of careful study. "Perfection" in such issues as these is a moot point, of course, but many observers find Urbino to possess a certain ambience of balanced forces and a high level of refinement. Although it is not possible to prove in a quantifiable way, it would be difficult to deny that there is a certain kind of perfection there.

The first entry in the journal from a visit to Urbino reads: "Thursday, June 11—approached Urbino from Rome in early evening. A remarkable view of the town from this vantage point, about 1500 meters s.w. of the gate through the wall beneath the palace. At this time of evening the sun illuminates the city from this direction and provides a remarkable introduction to the town."

6-11-81

Metropolitan Basilica

"new" south front of the Palazzo Ducale

the ramp "Platform" (i.e., Mercatale)

Francesco di Giorgio

URBINO
fm s-w

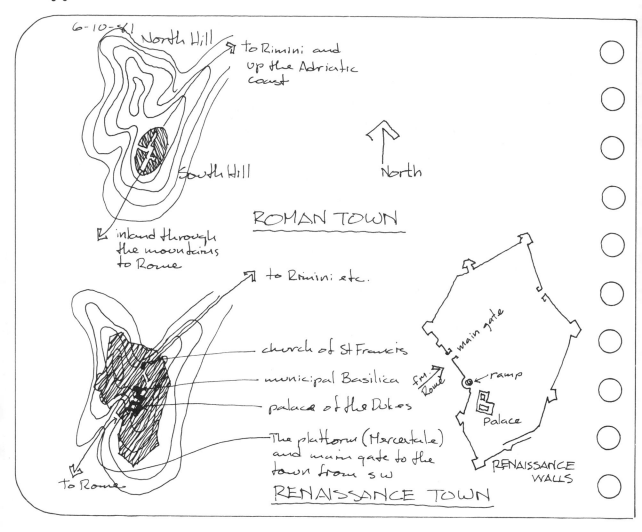

6-10-81 North Hill to Rimini and up the Adriatic coast

South Hill

inland through the mountains to Rome

North

ROMAN TOWN

to Rimini etc.

church of St Francis

municipal Basilica

palace of the Dukes

The platform (Mercantile) and main gate to the town from sw

to Rome

main gate

fm. Rome

ramp

Palace

RENAISSANCE WALLS

RENAISSANCE TOWN

The next journal entry outlined the history of this place and provided some explanation of its form and circumstances. Although these verbal notes were lengthy and detailed, it is only important here to grasp the essential characteristics which conditioned the exploration of the town. Especially important to understanding the form of the town is to be able to equate what one can see there today with the historical circumstances which created this form. Notes concerning how the city began as a Roman town on the south hill, spread to the north hill in medieval times, and how Renaissance architects helped to join the two parts by embellishing the piazza which lay in the saddle between them, were drawn from history and guidebooks and placed in the journal along with corresponding plan drawings of the town. Also included in the journal though not reproduced here, were references to a good restaurant, the location of two principal hotels, notes on paintings displayed in the Ducal Palace and so forth. In other words, the journal has become a working tool for exploring the town. It holds practical as well as esoteric information, some of which was recorded in the notebook before leaving for the Urbino visit, and it provides space for collecting information in the form of drawings, diagrams, notes, etc. during the course of the exploration. The journal, used in this way, is a comprehensive tool, and not *just* a document for later reference. The notebook used for the journal is seen as a necessary accoutrement to travel along with passport, traveler's checks, guidebooks, and umbrella.

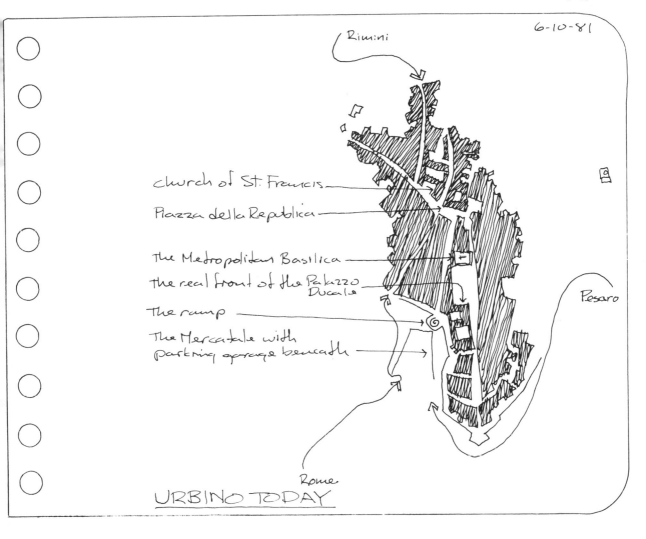

6-10-81

Rimini

church of St. Francis
Piazza della Republica

The Metropolitan Basilica
The real front of the Palazzo Ducale

The ramp

The Mercatale with parking garage beneath

Pesaro

Rome

URBINO TODAY

Urbino, like many other Italian provincial centers, is built atop a hill, actually atop two hills with a slight saddle between them. The town's main square, the Piazza della Republica, is located in this slight saddle and, along with the adjacent church of St. Francis, acts as a sort of hinge between the two parts of town on the north and the south hills. This is not quite evident, however, from the vantage point described above. What makes this vantage point along the road from Rome so remarkable is the way in which the town builds up from the base of the hill to a culmination in the two turrets of the Palazzo Ducale, or Palace of the Dukes. Further, the starting place of this build-up of forms is accentuated by a broad platform at the base of the hill, marking the base of the old defensive walls and

providing a datum for the collection of architectural forms above it.

The town appears today essentially as it did in the Renaissance after architects of that period reconciled portions of the town with one another by their designs for certain buildings, circulation ways, walls, and open spaces. The map drawings were reproduced from information in two books to bring them together in the journal to facilitate a more comprehensive understanding of the town's form. Of particular importance is how the town was "reoriented" after the medieval period so that it faced the south toward the approach from Rome, and away from the route from Rimini, the most important approach for several hundred years prior.

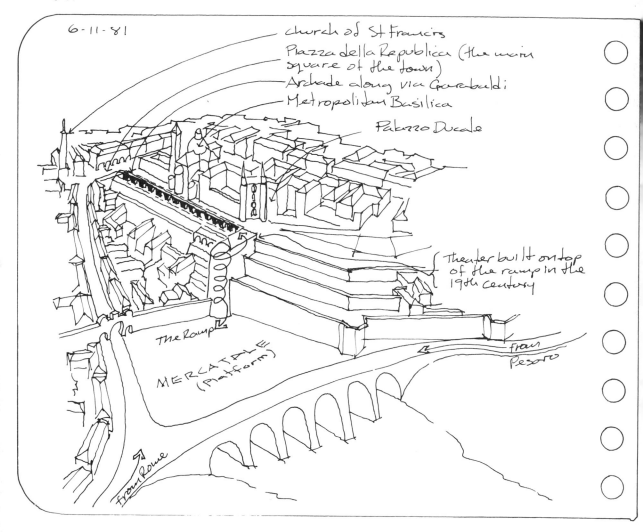

6-11-81

church of St Francis
Piazza della Republica (the main square of the town)
Arcade along Via Garabaldi
Metropolitan Basilica

Palazzo Ducale

Theater built on top of the ramp in the 19th century

The Ramp

MERCATALE (Platform)

from Pesaro

from Rome

Analytical drawings depicting the town as it can only be seen in the mind's eye help to explain the parts which were important to its reorientation in the Renaissance. This drawing shows how a platform was positioned across the valley to provide a "front porch" to the town as well as a convenient market square, and how the twin towers built onto the back of the Palazzo Ducale in the Renaissance offer a frontal gesture to anyone approaching from the southwest. This drawing is somewhat realistic, giving the texture, mass, and scale of the town as seen from afar, but it is not accurate in terms of detail. The number of buildings and their shapes and relationships with one another are approximate. Further, certain features are abstracted or exaggerated to

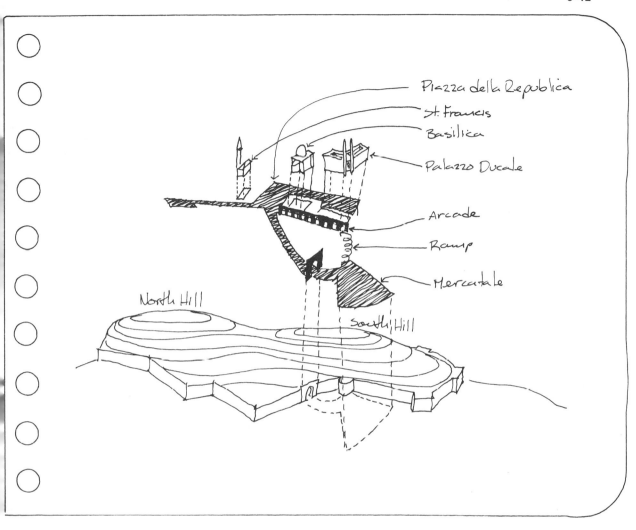

Piazza della Republica
St. Francis
Basilica
Palazzo Ducale

Arcade

Ramp

Mercatale

North Hill

South Hill

demonstrate their respective roles in the organization of the city.

A further abstraction singles out the important pieces, many of which were designed by the architect Francesco di Giorgio in the fifteenth century, and which still provide the principal organizing elements for the town. The Piazza della Republica acts as a hinge to the two sides of the town, located as it is in the saddle between the two hills. The arcade combined with the spiral ramp built by di Giorgio, connects the "front porch" with the main square in one way, and a special gate in the wall coupled with a street which sweeps unobstructed up the hill connects it in another way. The two churches help mark the center and the

Palazzo Ducale makes its gesture over the market square while the defensive walls surround it all, unifying many details and forms. This rather simple drawing distills essential qualities and parts, revealing how they work with one another.

- A brick town! most unexpected in central Italy. The brown brick with its diminutive scale (compared with stone masonry) gives the town a somewhat delicate character.
- Vistas: curving and angular streets close all vistas until one encounters a street which opens onto the landscape over the wall of the town. Then the scene is a dramatic suprise; typical of hill towns.

The next entries in the notebook came from an introductory walk through the town. This first walk around Urbino in the late afternoon light was intended to provide a general feel for the town, its internal organization, character from within, and impressions from its daily life. The verbal notes, sometimes in the form of exclamatory comments as above, record fresh impressions. Further notes regarding first impressions that afternoon record the setting for the town as seen from within, looking out. "The countryside is especially picturesque with countless little hills covered with a patchwork of crop fields, wood margins, vineyards and orchards. It reminds me of Grant Wood's paintings of Iowa, except here the fields are irregular in shape and the farm buildings are older, low brown brick structures with dusty red tile roofs. And, of course, the dotted patterns of vineyards punctuate the overall pattern."

The notes above record impressions concerning the town's organization as they are discovered. These verbal notes are concerned with the effect of the placement and use of various elements which condition the formal organization. Further notes, also verbal, which accompany the sketches, record something of the life of the town. "As evening comes on, the main square (Piazza della Republica) begins to fill with people, mostly students from the University. Tables and chairs appear to fill half the piazza. This is such a difference from when I first passed through the square three hours ago, with vehicles and people crisscrossed the piazza, seldom stopping."

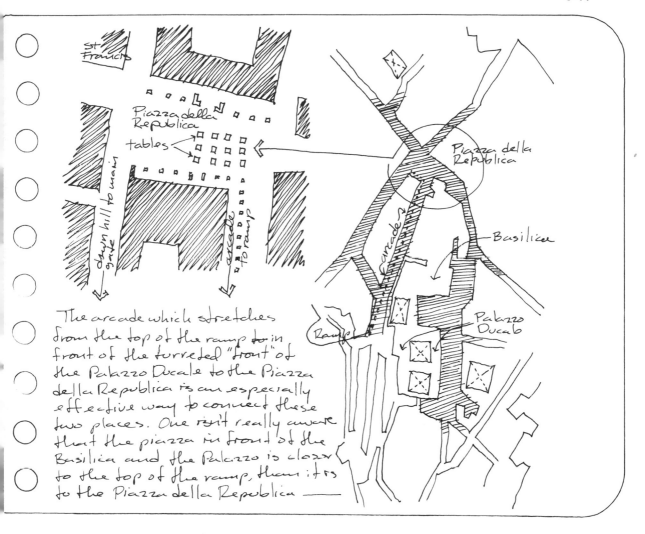

The arcade which stretches from the top of the ramp to in front of the turreted "front" of the Palazzo Ducale to the Piazza della Republica is an especially effective way to connect these two places. One isn't really aware that the piazza in front of the Basilica and the Palazzo is closer to the top of the ramp, than it is to the Piazza della Republica —

"The larger square in front of the Cathedral (Metropolitana Basilica) and the Palazzo Ducale is now almost deserted. It is clear that the Piazza della Republica is the one place to be in the cool of early evening."

An early comment recorded in this initial tour of the town, that the town is built of brick, is valuable because it records an impression before the observer has become used to characteristics which first impress visitors. First impressions as well as studied observations are of value since first impressions are an integral part of the whole experience and, hence, an integral part of a comprehensive understanding of the qualities of "place." Subsequent comments such as the one about the main square changing character markedly from

the daytime to the evening are based on studied observations which required comparatively lengthy exposure to the town. Each of these observations—the first impression and the temporal observation—is equally important in conveying salient characteristics of the town.

The observation about the route from the top of the Ramp, along the arcaded street and through the main square to the square

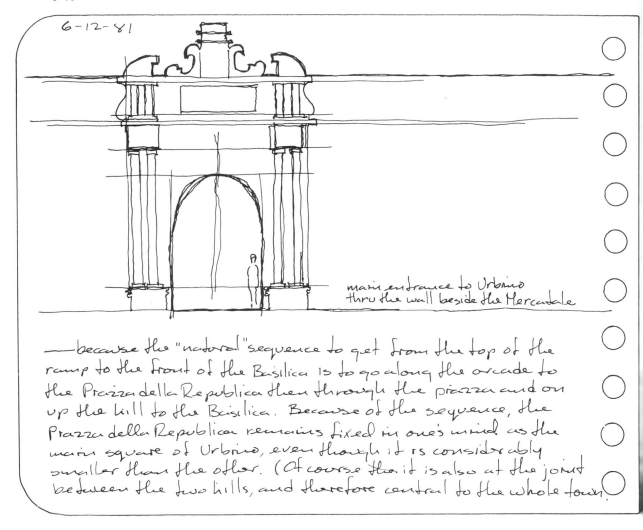

6-12-81

main entrance to Urbino
thru the wall beside the Mercatale

—because the "natural" sequence to get from the top of the ramp to the front of the Basilica is to go along the arcade to the Piazza della Republica then through the piazza and on up the hill to the Basilica. Because of the sequence, the Piazza della Republica remains fixed in one's mind as the main square of Urbino, even though it is considerably smaller than the other. (Of course that it is also at the joint between the two hills, and therefore central to the whole town)

of the Basilica (beginning on the previous notebook page and continuing above) is important for a number of reasons, but most of all because this sequence of spaces and how they are traversed helps to form one's understanding of the town's basic order. It could be said, as the notebook drawings illustrate, that the primary ordering characteristics of Urbino are:
1. the unifying quality of ubiquitous brown-brick walls and dusty red tile roofs;
2. the two hills with the main square as a conjunctive element placed between them;
3. the old defensive walls which completely surround and unify the town by making it appear as a completed object in the landscape (rather than if it were to spread out and disappear into the landscape without apparent edges as do most North American towns);

4. and finally there is this sequence of public spaces which link important places to one another in a coherent way.

The drawings which depict these ordering elements are particularly diagrammatic and nonpictorial in keeping with the conceptual nature of the ideas they represent.

These notes on Urbino were prompted by a certain attitude which conditioned the observations. One's approach to observations is usually guided by a predisposition toward the subject. This study of Urbino was made to gather notes which could be used in an article and to possibly inform an urban design scheme elsewhere. Preconceived notions of what is important and what is not might obscure valuable

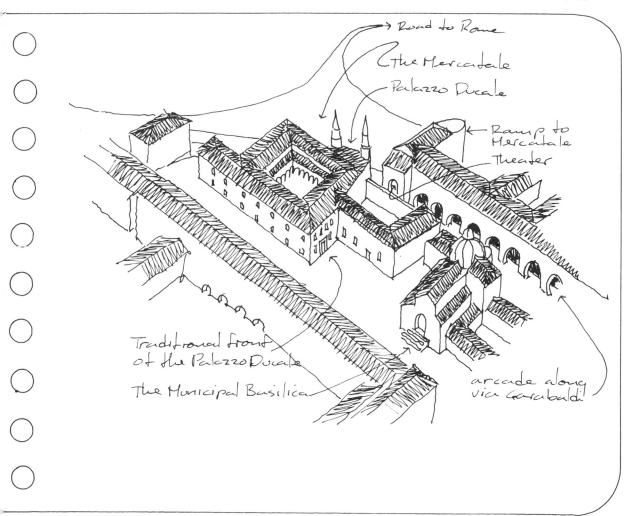

Road to Rome

The Mercatale

Palazzo Ducale

Ramp to Mercatale

Theater

Traditional front of the Palazzo Ducale

The Municipal Basilica

arcade along via Garabaldi

observations which do not fit the mold. However, if you are to approach a scene as richly complex as a city as though you were "an empty cup awaiting fulfillment," chances are that you will wander aimlessly with relatively little reward. It is in the act of careful selection that discoveries are made. A scientist forms an hypothesis, then proceeds to test his hypothesis against realities in the form of experimentation. Like the scientist, we make observations and record them based upon "an hypothesis" as to what is of value to seek out and record. In the process of doing so we enhance our experience, begin to observe emerging patterns, and discover faults in our premises. The discovery of faulty premises begs rethinking in much the same way as a scientist readjusts his

hypothesis before returning to further experimentation. The act of effective observation involves a dialectic between premises and observations. That could be seen to encourage narrow-mindedness, but if you approach your exploration with a point of view, you will have the discipline of focused observation to rely upon, giving you the freedom to wander about without danger of losing the force of purpose.

We hope this account of a visit to Urbino demonstrates how keeping visual notes can sharpen the observer's sense of observation. Each experience of note-taking sharpens one's capacity for observation, permitting a deeper penetration into the richness of complex places.

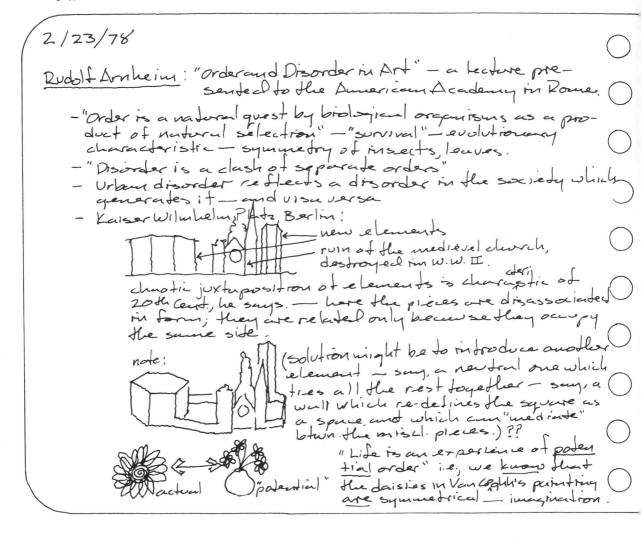

2/23/78

Rudolf Arnheim: "Order and Disorder in Art" — a lecture presented to the American Academy in Rome.

- "Order is a natural quest by biological organisms as a product of natural selection" — "survival" — evolutionary
characteristic — symmetry of insects, leaves.
- "Disorder is a clash of separate orders"
- Urban disorder reflects a disorder in the society which
generates it — and visa versa
- Kaiser Wilmhelm Platz, Berlin:

  new elements
  ruin of the medieval church,
  destroyed in W.W. II.

chaotic juxtaposition of elements is charistic [charactic] of
20th Cent, he says. — here the pieces are disassociated
in form; they are related only because they occupy
the same side.

note: (solution might be to introduce another
element — say, a neutral one which
ties all the rest together — say, a
wall which re-defines the square as
a space, and which can "mediate"
btwn the misc. pieces.) ??

"Life is an experience of potential order" i.e., we know that
the daisies in Van Gogh's painting
are symmetrical — imagination.

actual   "potential"

Attempting to capture the essential characteristics of a whole town such as Urbino is a formidable task made more nearly possible through visual notation. The same notebook-journal used to record observations in Urbino also contains fragments and thoughts from fleeting instances. In February of 1978 Rudolf Arnheim presented a lecture to the American Academy in Rome entitled "Order and Disorder in Art."[10] Notes from this lecture occupy one page of the journal, a bare fragment compared to Urbino. Captured from his slide lecture were illustrations concerning the relationship between visual "orderliness," i.e., obvious orders such as axial symmetry, and conceptual order, which Professor Arnheim called "potential" order, order which we know is there but do not necessarily see. He spoke of the importance of knowing such order was there even when it is not obvious to the eye because the knowledge we have of an underlying order helps to satisfy an innate quest for understanding order generally. We have included this page of the journal for two reasons. First, it contrasts with the foregoing case study by its verbal emphasis and brevity. Secondly, it suggests how distant observations can be brought together by a journal so that they can accomplish more than they might if they were to remain as totally separated ideas.

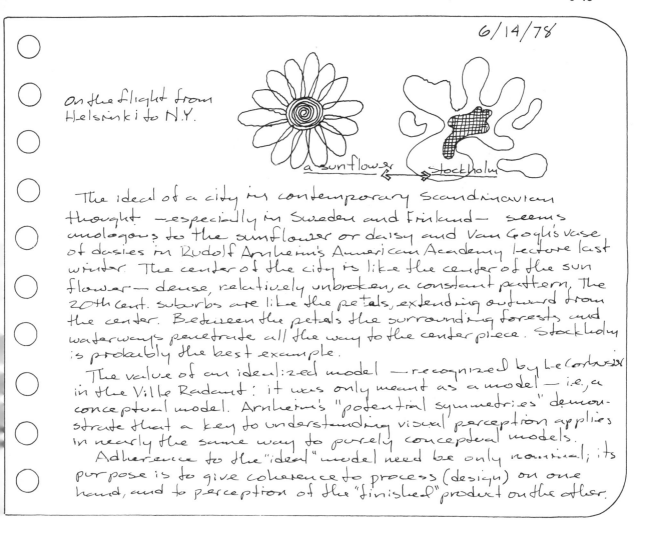

6/14/78

on the flight from Helsinki to N.Y.

a sunflower   Stockholm

The ideal of a city in contemporary Scandinavian thought —especially in Sweden and Finland— seems analogous to the sunflower or daisy and Van Gogh's vase of dasies in Rudolf Arnheim's American Academy lecture last winter. The center of the city is like the center of the sun flower— dense, relatively unbroken, a constant pattern. The 20th cent. suburbs are like the petals, extending outward from the center. Between the petals the surrounding forests and waterways penetrate all the way to the center piece. Stockholm is probably the best example.

The value of an idealized model —recognized by Le Corbusier in the Ville Radant: it was only meant as a model — i.e., a conceptual model. Arnheim's "potential symmetries" demonstrate that a key to understanding visual perception applies in nearly the same way to purely conceptual models.

Adherence to the "ideal" model need be only nominal; its purpose is to give coherence to process (design) on one hand, and to perception of the "finished" product on the other.

Reflections

This latter point is further illustrated by a page from the journal dated in June of that same year. After a visit to Stockholm with an architect who is responsible for helping to coordinate the planning efforts of governmental bodies with overlapping jurisdictions, it appeared that one idea behind city planning and urban design in this part of the world had to do with the importance of conceptual models. This recalled Arnheim's discussion of conceptual order in works of art as satisfying a "need" to know what is going on, which is as important for understanding a city as it is for a painting. This observation prompted connecting Arnheim's micro-scale observation with larger scale strategies for controlling and, especially, humanizing, the growth of cities. In this instance we recall Edward Fischer's statement that "a good reason to keep a journal is to have the consolation of seeing patterns form." These instances do not quite form a pattern, but it is possible to see one beginning here.

This study is like that of Urbino and is concerned with a similar group of issues. It looks at how new buildings have been accommodated in a district of an American city. Especially, it records attempts to integrate the new with the old in a way that is sensitive to the spirit, or *genius loci*, of that place.

Cities are complicated. No matter how large or small, they are composed of complexly interrelated social patterns, buildings, outdoor spaces, circulation systems for people and vehicles, and so forth. Street maps and verbal descriptions can only begin to record what is there. In the previous case study visual notes aided the understanding of a small, compact Italian town. Here a similar attempt is made

to understand something of the inner workings of a segment of a large American city. The note-taker is interested in solving problems of introducing new housing among existing housing patterns. The journey to Philadelphia to see this group of housing units came in response to seeing photographs of the completed project in a professional journal. Accompanying the photographs was a text which spelled out the apparent success of the complex with descriptive details and accompanying statistical data. However, a fully effective understanding of architecture and urban design cannot be gleaned from photographs, words, and numbers alone. Most of those qualities of the work which demonstrate principles of organization that can be translated into other work can only

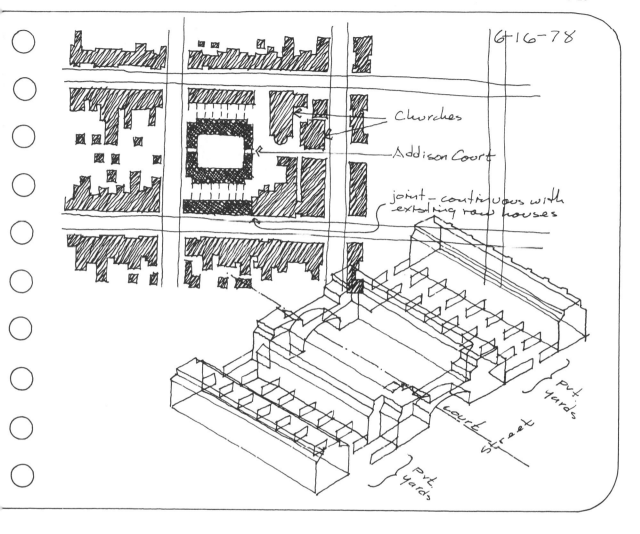

6-16-78

Churches

Addison Court

joint - continuous with
existing row houses

Pvt.
yards

court street

Pvt.
yards

be conveyed through the medium of graphic abstractions.

The complex, called Addison Court, was designed in 1968 by the Philadelphia architectural firm of Bower and Fradley; it consists of thirty-three units of housing set within an urban fabric composed of eighteenth century rowhouses aligning the streets in both directions, interrupted here and there by larger buildings such as churches and commercial structures. The complex of new housing units encloses an exterior open court which opens onto the streets on the east and west sides of the site through generous arched gateways, while facing the streets to the north and south with the repetitive facades of individual housing units. The houses are built

of red brick with windows and doors of painted wood. What makes this complex of particular interest is that it demonstrates some of the means by which new buildings set within an existing urban complex can be made to respond to their urban site, as a building in a natural landscape can be designed to respond to its surroundings.

If the observer could hover high above the site, he would be able to see how the new work has been integrated with the old. Based upon this, the first drawing is a plan of the district in which the new housing was placed. This drawing and the others in this study were done very quickly on the site in soft pencil, to be gone over with a fine point flow pen or fountain pen in the comfort of a hotel room in the evening of

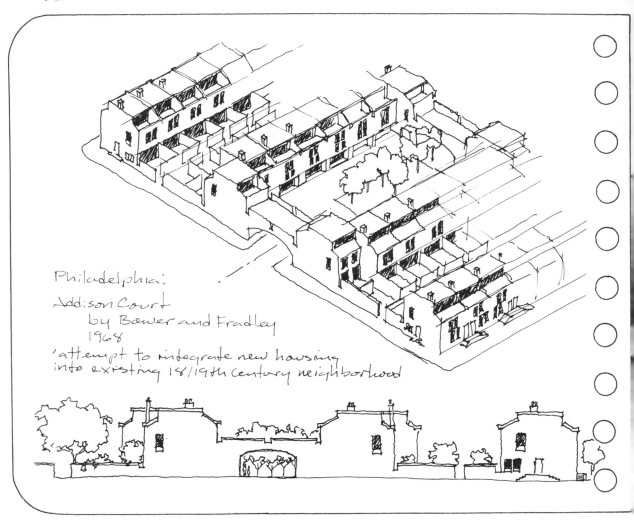

Philadelphia:
Addison Court
     by Bower and Fradley
     1968
'attempt to integrate new housing
into existing 18/19th Century neighborhood

the same day while the details were still fresh in mind. The pencil lines were then removed with a soft eraser, leaving the crisper and more purposeful lines to describe the forms and their relationships with one another.

The tiny site plan was constructed by generalizing the configuration of existing buildings after a drive around the neighborhood in a car. This was followed by a walk in the immediate area of the new work. The drawing shows how the new complex fits into the existing urban fabric. While some of the units continue the existing lines of rowhouses, others front upon a common enclosed court which forms a public space that is entirely unique to the neighborhood. Although it is unique it does not disrupt the existing pattern of outdoor spaces and related buildings which had perpetuated a delicate pattern of a social relationship and customs here for nearly two hundred years. Only a drawing which depicts the continuous open space defined by the buildings can explain the phenomenon of interplay between public spaces (streets and sidewalks) and semi-public ones (courts, alleys and parklike spaces such as church yards and school yards), and private spaces (such as the backyards of rowhouses).

Next, the exploration moved closer to capture the detailed relationships between new architecture and the old structures. An isometric drawing of the complex is con-

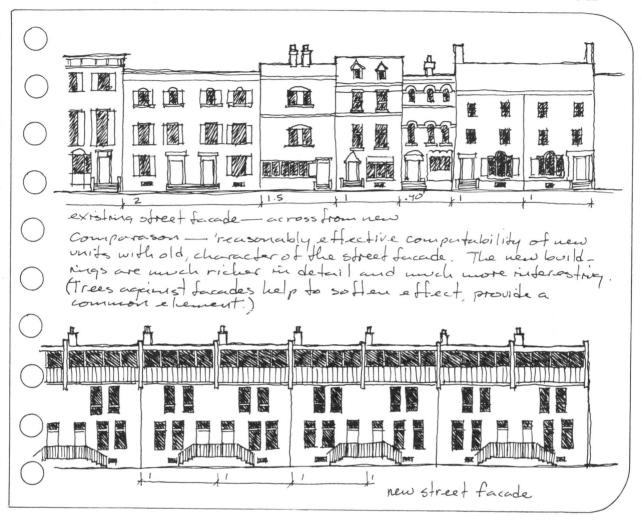

existing street facade — across from new

Comparason — 'reasonably effective computability of new units with old, character of the street facade. The new buildings are much richer in detail and much more interesting. (Trees against facades help to soften effect, provide a common element.)

new street facade

structed so as to appear transparent. This drawing depicts how built forms (walls, facades, gates, and the like) subdivide private spaces from one another, and how these spaces are subdivided from the more public ones; it also explains the basic structure of exterior space as designed by the project's architects. A larger scale isometric sketch (opposite) of the near corner of the complex shows how garden walls, window openings, gates, and stoops all work together in detailed relationships. It would be unnecessary to continue this detailed sketch further, since it can easily be related to the full isometric giving a sufficient overall impression of the entire complex.

In addition to these three drawings depicting the integration of the new with the old and parts of the new with each other, other drawings were done to capture another important quality of the group as set into an existing context. These elevations depict the sense of unity of the building group and consequent feeling of security within the larger neighborhood evoked by the more or less continuous wall on the east and west sides. The profile line, a suggestion of trees in yards and in the court beyond, and the punctures in the walls by window openings which are relatively small in relation to overall wall provide those features which characterize our "reading" of the grouping from without.

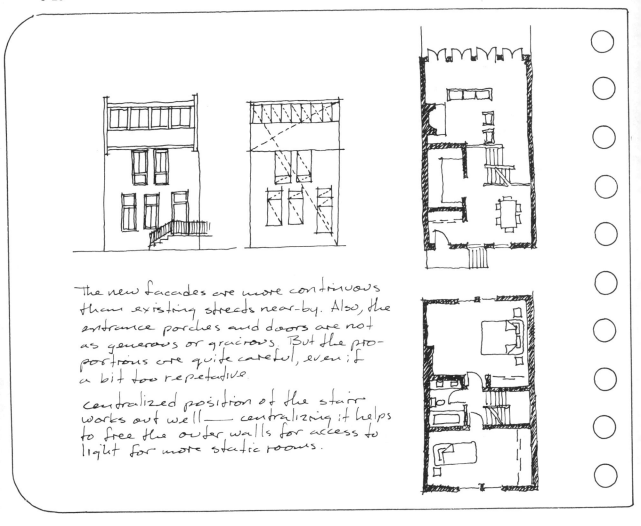

The new facades are more continuous than existing streets near-by. Also, the entrance porches and doors are not as generous or gracious. But the proportions are quite careful, even if a bit too repetative.

centralized position of the stair works out well — centralizing it helps to free the outer walls for access to light for more static rooms.

This last group of drawings, taken as notes on the site, are concerned with the disposition and character of the individual units which lie within the complex. Floor plans were sketched during a visit to a "model" unit. The arrangement and distribution of rooms, their relative sizes, the transition spaces between rooms, circulation spaces, provisions for storage and the like cannot be understood in a comprehensive way without such drawings. Note, by the way, how furniture has been included in these drawings to indicate the uses for each room and provide a sense of scale for the drawing itself. A more complete understanding of these relationships is further enhanced by the three-dimensional drawings which remove parts of the unit so that we can see into them. The very act of creating these drawings imparts an understanding of the inner workings of the units which could not otherwise be accomplished. Drawing a unit as though it were cut in two, extracting the vertical circulation for separate illustration, or pulling a unit out from between the repetitive party walls requires careful observation and thoughtful reconstruction in order to be reproduced with reasonable accuracy. The act of making these drawings, of figuring out how the units go together, is as important for understanding as the resultant visual notes are for preserving the information for later reference.

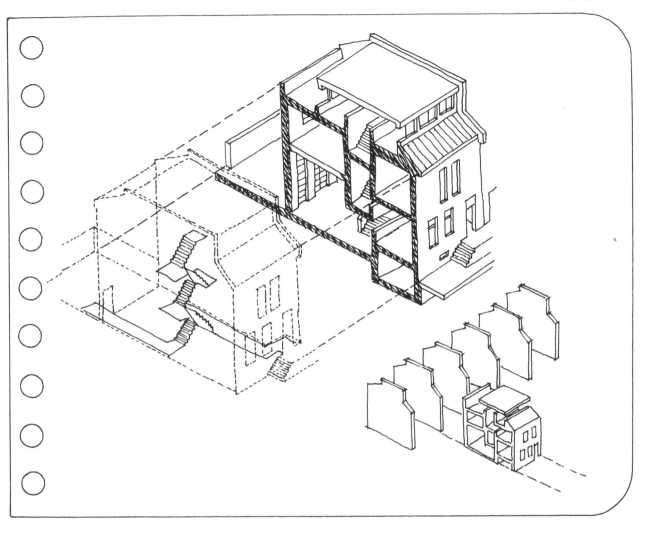

Of particular importance in this case study is how certain kinds of drawings were invented to analyze and record needed explanation. The transparent drawing of the overall complex, the pull-apart drawings of a particular unit, or the ghost facade with diagonal lines illustrating proportional elements through the superimposition of similar right triangles demonstrate how each drawing is tailored to the information which is intended to be conveyed. This approach, along with simplicity and economy of line for the sake of brevity and succinctness, distinguishes what we are calling visual notation from other approaches to drawing. The direct, no-nonsense purposefulness of each drawing satisfies a clear need for understanding and recording specific qualities at each instance. Each visual note depicts, through analysis, a very select range of information about the conditions being studied.

Visual notes provide a means for exploration. The sort of expansion they facilitate is one of depth as well as breadth. Taking visual notes often reveals that there is much more to what is being seen than first meets the eye. This case study explores one of the oldest residential parks in Paris. The park appears to be as simple as the diagram from which it was derived. It is a square, surrounded by houses and filled with trees. It is approached from one street which crosses the square from the northeast to northwest corners of the square and two other streets which penetrate below the houses at the middle of the north and south sides of the square. This appearance of simplicity is, however, an illusion. If one were to design a new park which was based on this one, from such a superficial

knowledge of it, the new design would not come close to achieving the success of the Place des Vosges. This famous square in the Marais district of Paris is a nice place to spend a quiet afternoon, and it was from such an afternoon that these notes began. In order to understand the success of this urban space it is necessary to see it in relation to the basic element which makes urban spaces—parks, piazzi, squares, etc.—successful, that is, the presence of people. Why are they there, why so many and, especially, why such a variety: old, young, local residents, tourists, shopkeepers, office workers, mothers with their children? The answers are many and have to do with numerous factors including how the park is policed, maintained and administered, the make-up of the surrounding

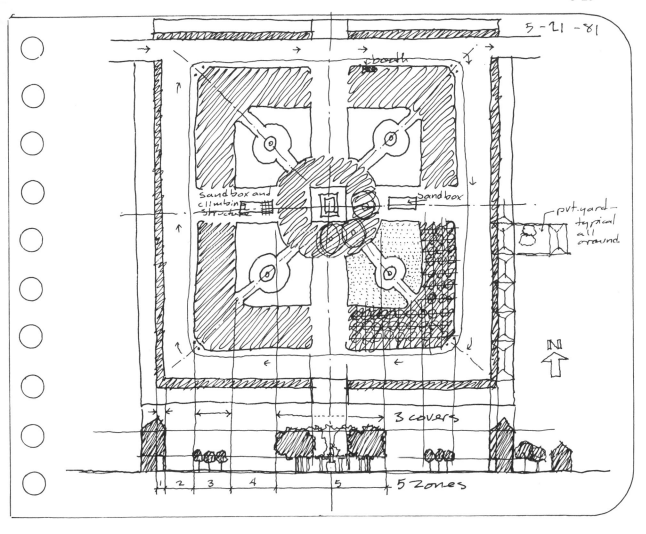

population, and the attitudes of Parisians regarding coming together in public places for recreation and relaxation. Although not seeking to diminish the importance of administrative and sociological functions, we will concentrate here upon those physical and visual qualities that make this place successful.

The deceptive simplicity of this special space begins to dissipate as one recognizes how its constituent parts work together like the intricate patterns of shape and color woven into a tapestry. For instance, although the park is filled with trees, the trees are planted in geometric patterns which provide the park with an array of roomlike spaces and open corridors that offer variety among places within the

parent place for special uses and special moods at different times of day and seasons of the year. The houses which surround the square not only define it as a special place within the city, but they also crisply delineate its extent, provide cool loggias at its periphery, and impose a stately and dignified urban quality on the whole ensemble. Appropriately, the first visual notation recorded is one which traces the overall organization of the space, the geometry to which everything is subservient and which provides the medium through which all constituent parts work with one another.

This first sketch was made on site and is dense with guidelines, verbal notes, and numbers. The second is a more careful

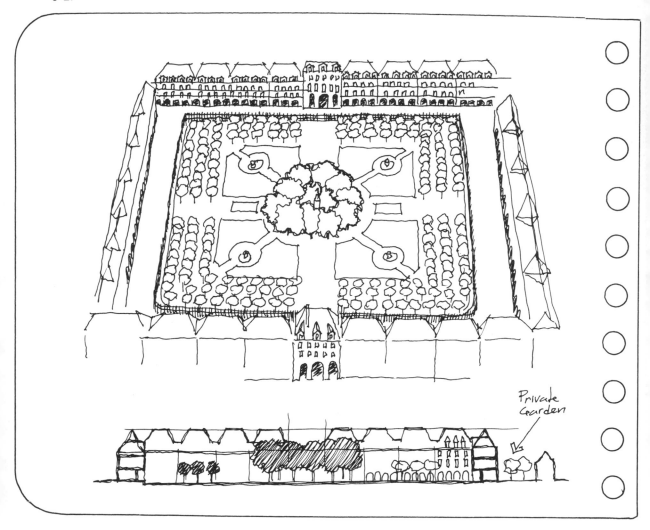

Private Gearden

drawing, based upon the first but done in pencil and gone over with a pen in the evening back at the hotel on the first day. The first drawing is the more important one. It displays the procedure involved in its creation by leaving the layout lines which were necessary to make the drawing, and thereby describes the salient characteristics of the park's basic order. The second drawing is more pleasing to look upon and was done to depict certain details and the relative sizes of things which must be shown three-dimensionally to adequately understand them. Returning to the first drawing again, it is important to note that the section drawn just below the plan is critical to understanding how the trees and the surrounding buildings form spaces of varying character. The act of

making this section drawing prompted a further investigation into the specific properties of the section which account for the varying special characteristics within the park. This resulted in still another drawing which records the ratios of width for the respective zones articulated by the loggias of surrounding houses, the street in front of them, the small low trees planted in three tight rows, and the broad open space which separates the triple row of trees from the mass of big trees at the center of the park. Miscellaneous sketches of people enjoying the park demonstrate how people respond to the broad open places, the quiet "avenues," and the darkly shaded quiet places with their comfortable benches. Clearly, the two space-defining elements, buildings and trees, provide the real

substance of the park's character. The trees in combination with the arcades form three concentric rings of covered exterior space protected from the rain and the more intense brightness of the sun. The innermost ring is composed of large trees with a spread of 60 to 70 feet, providing a thick canopy over the central area. The three rows of trees in the next ring have a spread of 15 to 20 feet in diameter and provide shelter and shade for benches; because of their alignments, they form pedestrian "boulevards" to walk among, or for bench-sitters to watch those walking. Finally, there are the houses at the outer edge with their arcades. The houses are screened from the park by a decorative fence which has gates at the corners and midpoints that are locked at night and opened in the morn-

ing by the park's attendants. The arcades at trees in their own way with the repetitive cadence of their arches and piers played against the even spacing of tree trunks and arched canopies of leaves and branches. The houses are stately and urbane and their facades relatively uniform in order to unify the space they define. To relieve the monotony that their uniformity might otherwise produce, the line is punctuated by the royal residences which straddle the mid-square entry points on the north and south sides of the square. Drawings depicting these buildings were made from vantage points on benches within the park; they attempt to describe the ordering principles which regulate the house's facades, just as the plan drawings of the park describe its ordering geometrics.

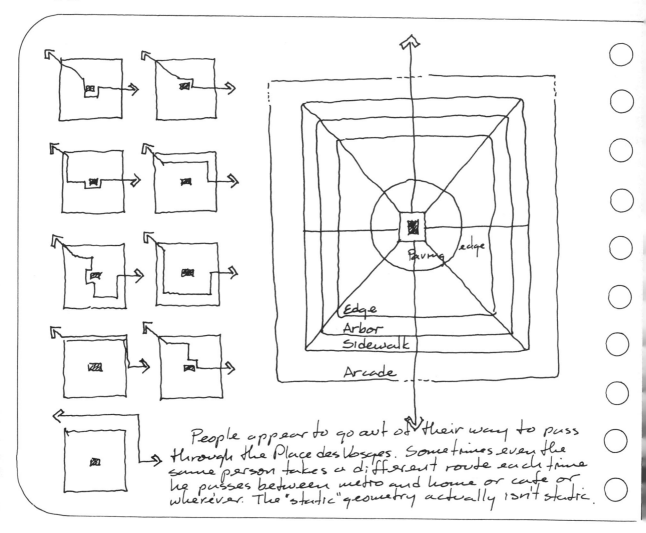

People appear to go out of their way to pass through the Place des Vosges. Sometimes even the same person takes a different route each time he passes between metro and home or cafe or wherever. The "static" geometry actually isn't static.

A day spent in the Place des Vosges reveals that one ingredient of the activity within the square derives from its convenience as a passage for people on their way across the Marais district, particularly those people going to and from the subway or market. Enroute they might stop for a cup of coffee and a bit of conversation at one of the cafes in the surrounding arcades or to read their newspaper on a bench among the trees where they can observe one another casually over the tops of their papers without seeming to ogle or intrude. Many, however, traverse the park without stopping. If you sit and watch people cross the space from corner to side, side to side, or whatever, it becomes clear that not everyone takes the same route between the same entry and exit points. One person

might take a different route each time he crosses the square. This observation prompted the drawing which depicts some of the various paths one can follow if one chooses to use the park as part of one's journey; it shows how the geometry of the square encourages a variety of experiences as a pedestrian typically follows one component of the geometry and then another.

This case study makes use of realistic drawings of people using the place being investigated. They are presented here to demonstrate how skill in drawing people in a simple notational way can convey important qualities of a place. This skill is not easy to come by, of course, but if developed, it provides another effective notational device. Because these are

5-22-81

perspective drawings, they require a knowledge of optical principles and perspective layout, but learning these principles and techniques is not as difficult as it would seem and can be absorbed in a step-by-step procedure (see chapter 5).

Sometimes, effective visual notes cannot be easily read by someone other than the one who drew them. The same can be said for verbal notes, of course. We have selected sequences of notational sketches here so that they can be read easily by anyone who might pick up this book, but we trust that the "artistic skill" they seem to require will not deter anyone from making their own, perhaps less articulate notes.

3–31

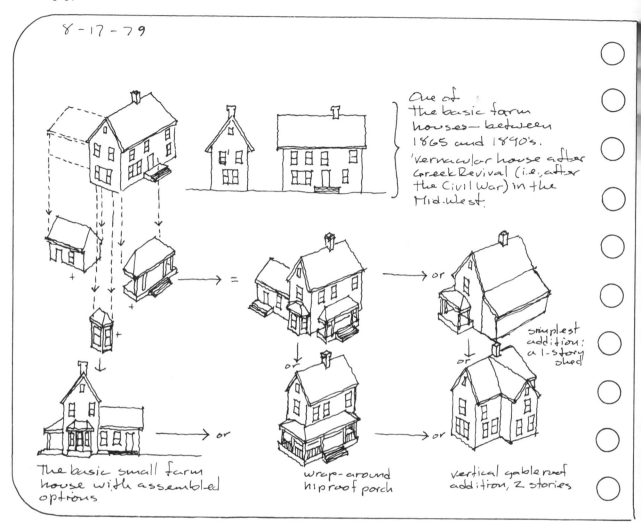

8-17-79

One of the basic farm houses— between 1865 and 1890's. 'Vernacular house after Greek Revival (i.e., after the Civil War) in the Mid-West.

The basic small farm house with assembled options

wrap-around hip roof porch

vertical gable roof addition, 2 stories

simplest addition: a 1-story shed

The Urbino, Philadelphia, and Place des Vosges case studies were explorations of special places with unique qualities. Their unity came about, in part, because they were each subject to the cultural influences of their place in the world. The following pages from the journal explore subjects scattered over a wide area. This time unity and coherence came about through consistency in the ideas which produced the pieces that these pages explore. The note-taker consciously brings together scattered remnants of a coherent pattern which is not easily discerned by casual observation. As

in the case of discovering a tie between a lecture at the American Academy in Rome and the long-range planning proposals for Stockholm, this set of notes ties together separate experiences. This time, however, an hypothesis precedes the exploration, and the visual notes substantiate and expand upon basic assumptions.

These notes were made in response to a bus trip across Iowa in 1973 necessitated by an airline employee's strike. The slow ride permitted the observation that midwest farm houses and barns built up through the

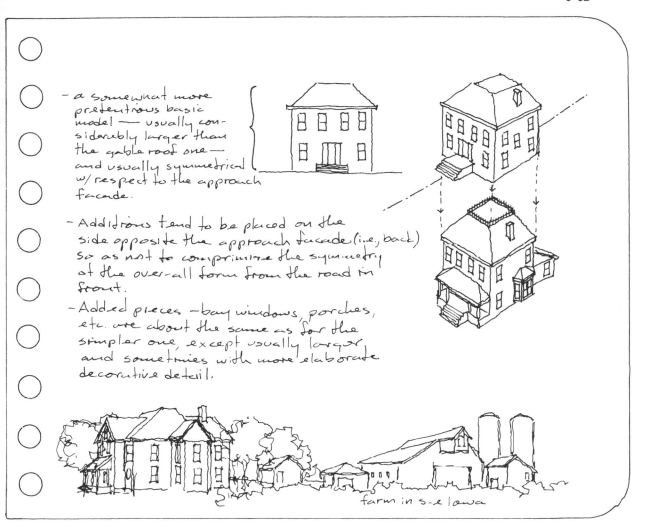

- a somewhat more
pretentious basic
model — usually con-
siderably larger than
the gable roof one —
and usually symmetrical
w/ respect to the approach
facade.

- Additions tend to be placed on the
side opposite the approach facade (i.e., back)
so as not to comprimize the symmetry
of the over-all form from the road in
front.

- Added pieces — bay windows, porches,
etc. are about the same as for the
simpler one, except usually larger,
and sometimes with more elaborate
decorative detail.

farm in s-e Iowa

1920s appear to be related in an intricate pattern of form, shape, and detail. Not only are they usually built of the same materials in the same way, and painted white, but they are obviously all a part of a surprisingly intricate "system."

The first two journal pages explore the two basic "models" upon which all farm houses along the journey seem to be based. One is rather small, delicate, and asymmetrical, apparently for farmers who began very modestly. The other is more spacious from the start and is often symmetrical. The larger one with its symmetrical front facing the road probably satisfied certain desires for stature and status. The most interesting revelation, however, has to do with how a basic "model," built from standard designs by carpenters or neighbors, could grow and change according to the owner's needs and means. Various pieces, such as a bay window, hip and gable roof porches, room additions and so forth, could be combined to satisfy very specific needs while always ensuring, it seems, a harmonious ensemble, apparently complete at any stage of expansion. A close look at these houses reveals

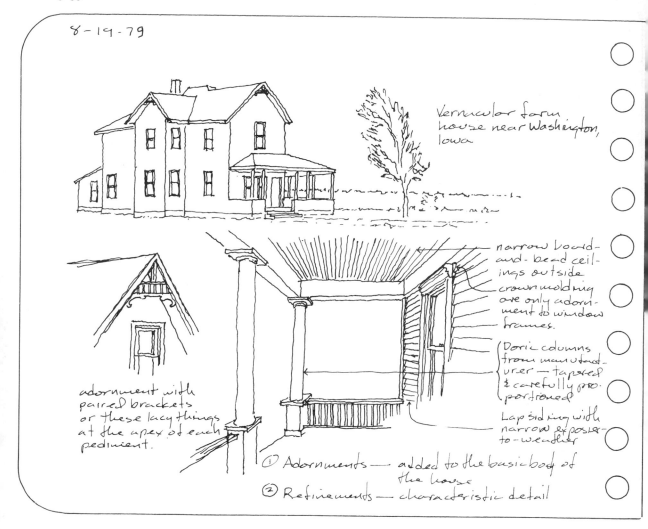

8-19-79

Vernacular farm house near Washington, Iowa

narrow board-and-bead ceil-ings outside crown molding are only adorn-ment to window frames.

Doric columns from manufact-urer — tapered & carefully pro-portioned

Lap siding with narrow exposure-to-weather

adornment with paired brackets or these lacy things at the apex of each pediment.

① Adornments — added to the basic body of the house
② Refinements — characteristic detail

that the workmanship and construction for both models is essentially the same. In both, there is a remarkable concern for precision and detail. The plainest house is refined in all the necessary details, such as how the siding meets frames and how the undersides of porches and eaves are treated. Beyond the basics, decorative elements may appear, such as a delicate lace of wood caught at the top of a gable, but seldom does a house ever seem to be overdone and seldom do any of the embellishments ever seem to be out of place. Barns, like the houses, are based upon a basic model and subsequent expansions follow a consistent pattern. Once again the building never appears incomplete at any stage in its growth.

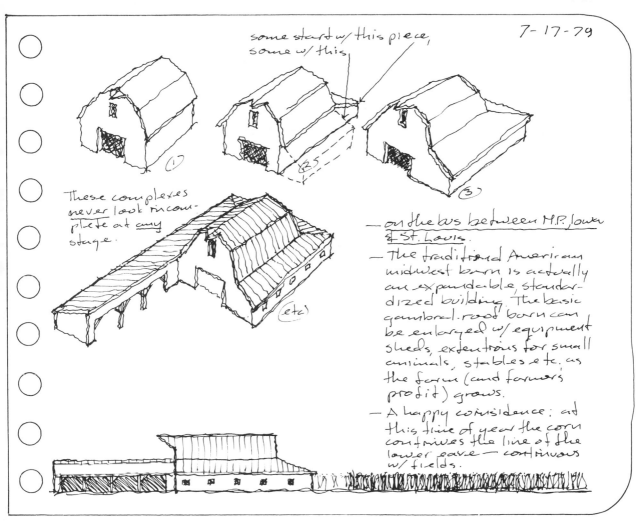

some start w/ this piece, some w/ this

7-17-79

① ② ③

These complexes never look incomplete at _any_ stage.

(etc)

— on the bus between M.P. Tower & St. Louis.
— The traditional American midwest barn is actually an expandable, standardized building. The basic gambrel-roof barn can be enlarged w/ equipment sheds, extentions for small animals, stables etc. as the farm (and farmer's profit) grows.
— A happy coincidence: at this time of year the corn continues the line of the lower eave — continuous w/ fields.

These notes were first drawn in pencil on the bus. The ride was too rough to allow for intelligible drawings, so they were redrawn later and elaborated upon as their redrawing spawned further thoughts on the subject. Due to the redrawing process and to the systematic nature of the subject, the drawings appear more as page illustrations than visual notation, but their origin was as hasty notation scribbled onto pages of note paper. In addition to demonstrating how visual notation can assemble scattered incidences into a relationship with one another to recreate the pattern of which they are a part, these notes demonstrate how skill in visual note-taking can take advantage of unforeseen circumstances.

3–35

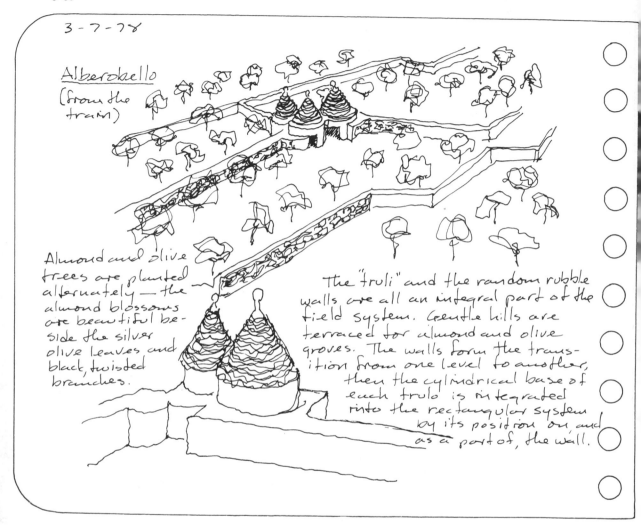

3-7-78

Alberobello
(from the
train)

Almond and olive trees are planted alternately — the almond blossoms are beautiful beside the silver olive leaves and black, twisted branches.

The "truli" and the random rubble walls are all an integral part of the field system. Gentle hills are terraced for almond and olive groves. The walls form the transition from one level to another, then the cylindrical base of each trulo is integrated into the rectangular system by its position on, and as a part of, the wall.

Observations such as those about American farm buildings can help to expand one's awareness of more general conditions of which they are an example. The drawings above are from a train ride in southern Italy across a part of the peninsula where Saracen immigrants settled hundreds of years ago. Farm houses and agricultural buildings are truly remarkable in their shape and in the way they fit into the elaborate field system. While farm buildings almost everywhere including North America tend to stand out as isolated groupings set beside their agricultural holdings, these houses and storage buildings are an integral part of the network of orchards. The walls which bound the fields and the buildings become as one, as though the buildings reach out to encompass fields, pastures, and groves.

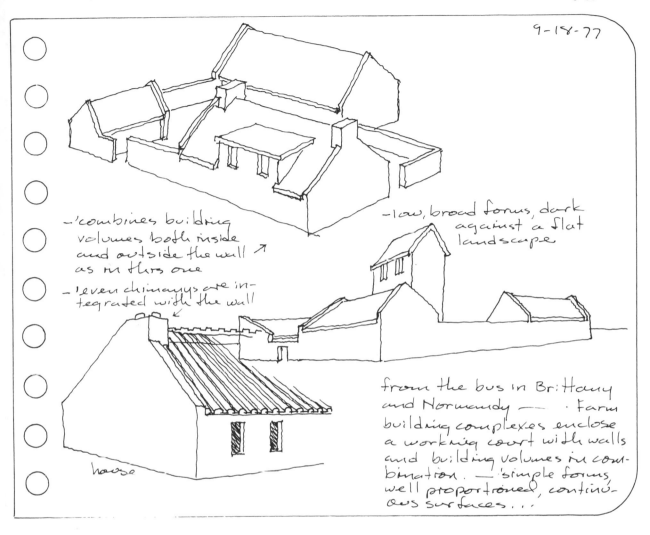

9-18-77

—'combines building
volumes both inside
and outside the wall ↗
as in this one

— 'even chimneys are in-
tegrated with the wall ↙

—low, broad forms, dark
against a flat
landscape

house

from the bus in Brittany
and Normandy — · farm
building complexes enclose
a working court with walls
and building volumes in combination. — 'simple forms,
well proportioned, continuous surfaces . . .

The last page of drawings of farm buildings also came from observations made from a bus window. This trip was across Normandy and Brittany. In this part of the world, traditional farm buildings are grouped about an enclosure to form a working courtyard with the residence, barns, service buildings, and a wall. The wall becomes integral with the buildings in an intriguing way; it is difficult to distinguish building wall from free-standing courtyard wall because the same wall serves both purposes.

These three observations, midwest farm buildings, southern Italian farm complexes, and farms in western France, were separated from one another by several years, but the journal brings them together so they may be compared or inform other investigations of help in solving related design problems.

**University of Virginia and the
Certosa di Pavia: Pursuing a
Persistent Pattern**

3-37

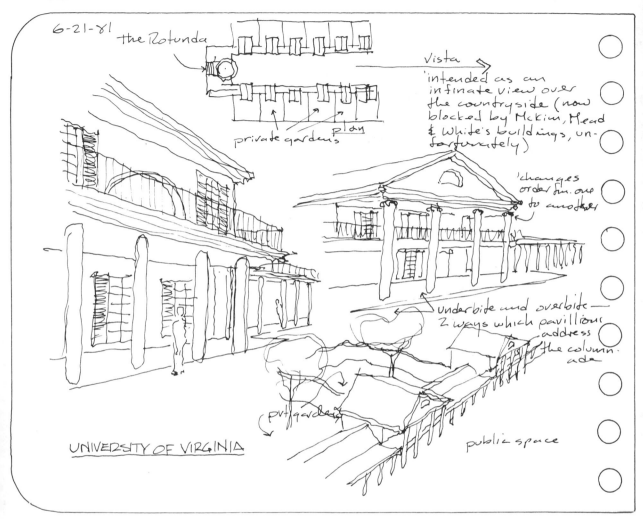

6-21-81   the Rotunda

vista
'intended as an
infinate view over
the countryside (now
blocked by Mckim, Mead
& White's buildings, un-
fortunately)

private gardens   plan

'changes
order fm. one
to another

underbite and overbite —
2 ways which pavillions
address
the column-
ade

(pvt gardens)

public space

UNIVERSITY OF VIRGINIA

The quality and character of drawings in anyone's journal would likely vary from one page to another. The level of precision and detail would respond to the requirements of the information being extracted and recorded and the amount of time one has to spend. The above page is similar to those that were originally drawn in pencil; but here the original drawings were done in pen and remain as they were set down, unamended.

The subject is the colonnade surrounding the original quadrangle at the University of Virginia, designed by Thomas Jefferson in 1817. As in the Place des Vosges, a large parcel of outdoor space is defined and given form by surrounding architecture. Here however the emphasis is directional

rather than centroidal. The focus of the University's quadrangle is an infinite vista across the rolling Virginia countryside; it is emphasized by a modestly monumental building, the Rotunda, positioned at the end opposite the vista and reinforced by the linear proportions of the space.

A sensitivity to structured outdoor spaces, fostered by the afternoon in the Place des Vosges, is responsible for the interest in Thomas Jefferson's design which provoked these sketches. A noteworthy discovery resulting from the investigation was the role of the columns in relation to the walls and the buildings along two sides of the quadrangular space.

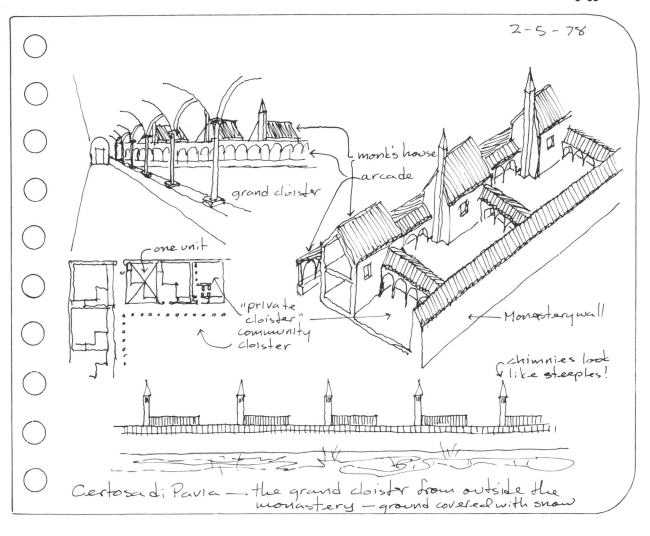

2-5-78

grand cloister

monk's house

arcade

one unit

"private cloister"
community cloister

Monastery wall

chimnies look like steeples!

Certosa di Pavia — the grand cloister from outside the monastery — ground covered with snow

A similar investigation occurred on an earlier page of the journal. A Renaissance monastery near Pavia, Italy, uses similar means to establish the boundary of its "grand cloister." The monastery, Certosa di Pavia, provides houses for each monk, similar to the professors' houses at the University of Virginia. The visual notes demonstrate how a means for arranging outdoor spaces of different sizes and levels of privacy can be achieved and how similar design approaches can be applied to apparently dissimilar circumstances with equally satisfactory results. The journal has once again helped to find a recurring pattern, theme, or motif.

3–39

This sequence of notational sketches is part of an investigation of the design for adaptive re-use of an historic building. The basic problem of adaptive re-use of existing buildings is an important one where the historic fabric of towns and cities is seen to be of significant value. Castelvecchio, in Verona, Italy, dates from the thirteenth century, and includes portions of a medieval church and Roman walls. It was converted to a museum in 1924 and fitted with pieces of old Verona palaces. It was bombed in 1945 and then re-designed and restored in 1958 by the Italian architect, Carlo Scarpa. Scarpa's design is a significant commentary upon architectural restoration and adaptation. It could even be seen as a modern counterpart, in theoretical terms, to Michaelangelo's adaptation of the Roman Baths of Diocletian for a Christian church. Embodied in this work by Scarpa are the basic questions concerning historical adaptations for architecture: what might be changed without destroying the connection with history, what ought to be preserved, and what should be restored to the way it once was. Scarpa's answer was to create an intricate collage of old, new, very old, and enigmatic; he thereby combined tangible remnants of two thousand years of Veronese history into one architectural complex in the midst of the city.

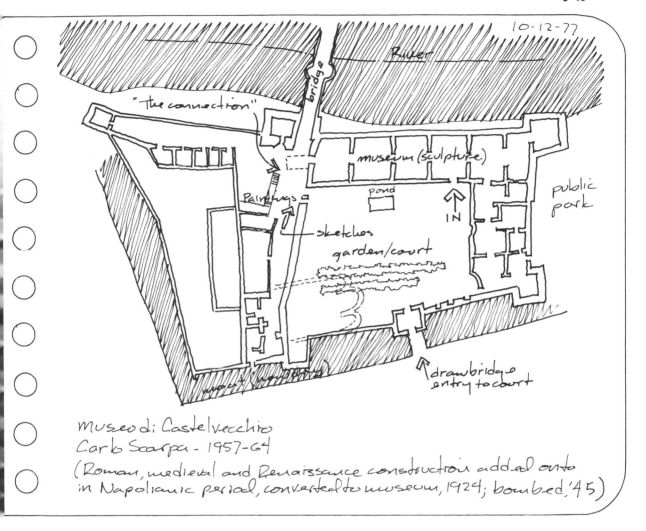

10-12-77

River

bridge

"the connection"

museum (sculpture)

pond

public park

Paintings

sketches
garden/court

IN

3

drawbridge
entry to court

Museo di Castelvecchio
Carlo Scarpa - 1957-64
(Roman, medieval and Renaissance construction added onto
in Napolianic period, converted to museum, 1924; bombed '45)

The notebook pages which document a visit to Castelvecchio include both quick sketchy notes and rather detailed, precise ones. The visit was rather brief—only a morning—and there was little time for elaborate drawings, and the dark rainy day prohibited any effective photography. Therefore, quick notes were drawn on the spot with a flow pen, and some detailed notes were laid out in pencil and gone over in ink at a later time. The plan of Castelvecchio was drawn from a diagram in a guidebook. It was done to gain a familiarity with the layout of elements and to have a record of it.

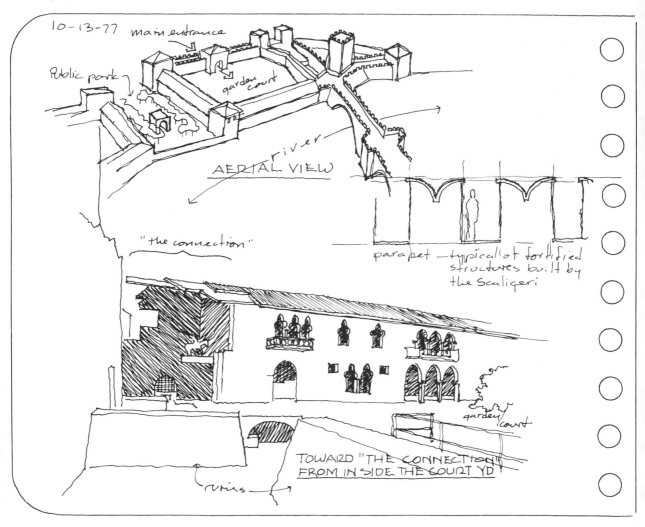

The aerial view was sketched after walking around the complex so that a more comprehensive understanding of the site might be gained. This exercise clarified the relationships between what was going on in adjacent courtyards and the primary site features such as neighboring urban fabric and the Adige River. The aerial view was surmised; this is not quite ideal, but is the best alternative to viewing the area from an aircraft.

The main wall of the museum's sculpture gallery is drawn in a rough sketch from a point referenced on the plan. The purpose of this drawing was to record the context for a sketch of the "connection," a place where the idea of a collage is most demonstratively developed. The close-up of the "connection" provides little more than an impression of this area, but that is its purpose. It demonstrates how the architect allowed a mixture of forces to come together at this juncture between the two primary parts of the old fortification and the entrance to the bridge, where fragments of Roman and medieval construction mingle with Renaissance and modern. Here he placed the equestrian statue of Can Grande, up in the air and askew of other geometries. It becomes a reminder of the Scaligers, the noble family whose history is most associated with this place.

"the connection" — a collage of parts, images, and Verona's history

"THE CONNECTION"

In the investigation of almost any building, what one sees becomes a combination of what one is looking for and what asserts itself upon the visitor regardless of original intentions. Besides the notion of intermingling pieces from across time in the form of an historical collage, two features of the present building speak persistently to a discerning visitor. One has to do with the subtle treatment of surfaces of walls, floors, ceilings, frames, and decorative elements. The other concerns the treatment of openings in walls and partitions. Surface treatment is difficult to convey in an effective way with visual notation because it relies upon color, texture, the innate qualities of materials, and the juxtaposition of these things. Openings in walls and partitions, however, became a major focus of

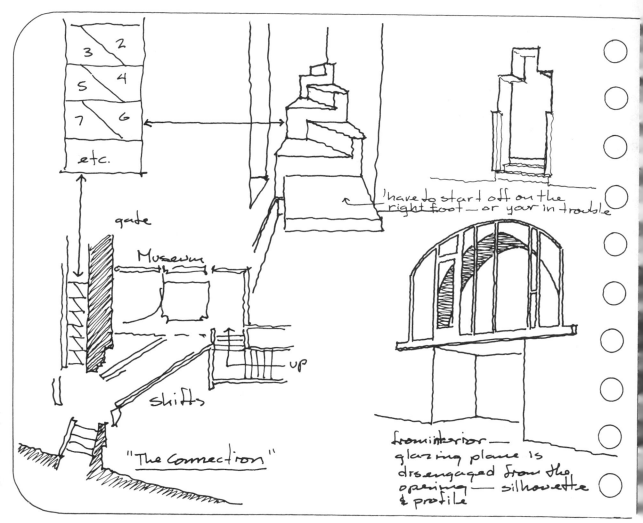

3 2
5 4
7 6
etc.

gate

Museum

shifts

"The Connection"

UP

'have to start off on the right foot — or your in trouble

from interior —
glazing plane is
disengaged from the
opening — silhouette
& profile

these notes. It was not the intention of the visit to focus upon this subject, but Carlo Scarpa's treatment of existing doors and windows, his approaches to modifying their function and to making new openings in existing walls proved to be one of the design's most informative aspects.

The issue with openings primarily concerns light and shape. An opening in a wall seen from within presents a silhouette of itself in brightness against a relatively dark wall. From without, that same opening presents a dark shape lying on the bright surface of the outside wall. In either case, the shape of the opening becomes dominant. In the museum, many openings in the outside wall which were formerly unglazed now had to be fitted with doors or glazing and window frames. The usual solution to framing an opening is to run a frame around the inside of the opening, which would modify the shape of the traditional unglazed opening. The architect's solution to this problem was to disassociate the glazing plane from the opening, thus preserving the opening's original profile while introducing a "layer" or plane of modern equipment along the inside surface of the ancient walls. This produced an interplay continuing the dialogue between old and new as is consistent with the theme of adaptation as a collage of apparently disparate elements.

In the drawings the real contrast of light-delineating profile cannot be accurately represented without elaborate, subtle shading, and the application of color.

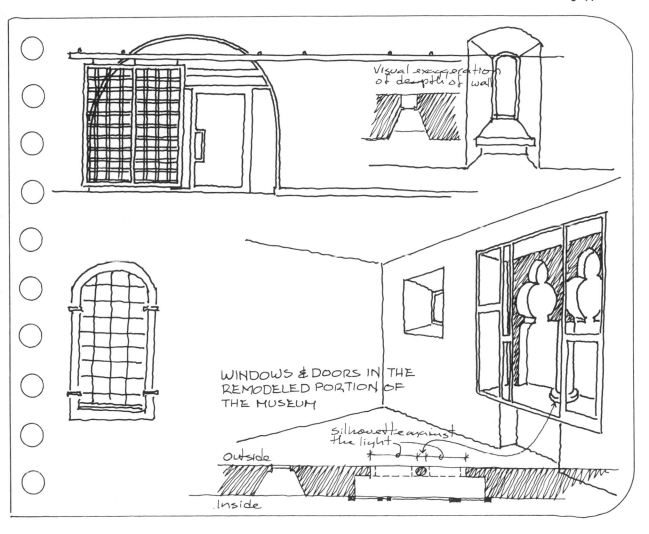

Visual exaggeration of depth of wall

WINDOWS & DOORS IN THE
REMODELED PORTION OF
THE MUSEUM

silhouette against
the light

Outside

Inside

Therefore, in some cases a simple verbal note must suffice, while in others, a scribbled shading on the glass (if outside, looking in) or on the surrounding wall (if inside, looking out) is used. In this case study, each drawing was done in a manner to match the appropriate condition of time and detail; some are sketchy and others relatively precise. In this regard, this case study is perhaps the most typical. The information that was recorded was discovered inadvertently through experiencing the architecture firsthand, by seeking out items which were known to be there beforehand, and by uncovering information through the process of drawing and note-taking. The unexpected treatment of openings was explored and can now serve as a basis for new comparative exploration elsewhere.

3-45

This case study follows from the last part of the investigation of Verona's Castel-vecchio. In the historic fortification, the windows were of particular interest because of their shape and the ties which that made to former historical cir-cumstances. This is only a narrow portion of the range of functions served by win-dows. In this case study, we focus upon this particular detail of buildings—win-dows—as a demonstration of how visual notation helps in gathering information about a particular subject from a variety of sources scattered over time and distance, so that conclusions may be drawn from what might otherwise remain separated and unassoclated observations and ideas.

Windows satisfy a remarkable number of tasks in a building. They let in light, control the flow of air in and out, direct views, and provide a pattern which lends stature and interest to the facades of buildings. Often the tasks they are to perform are conflict-ing. They must admit the direct rays of the sun during the winter to help warm the in-terior, but keep them out in the summer while still admitting light and permitting views from within. In this sequence of notes, the author has sought out designs for windows which best satisfy the broadest possible range of functions. The investigation of windows was accom-plished in preparation for considering designs for new windows which are more effective in controlling the environment of a building's interior than is usual for windows

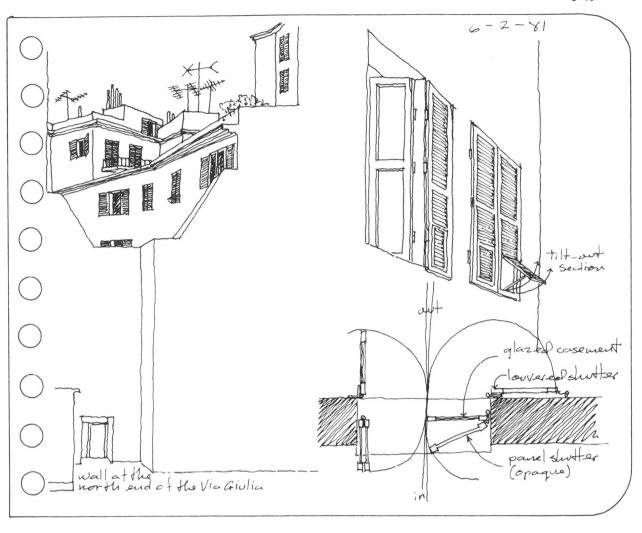

6-2-81

tilt-out
section

out

glazed casement

louvered shutter

panel shutter
(opaque)

in

wall at the
north end of the Via Giulia

in American buildings. In American buildings, it has been customary to rely heavily upon mechanical means (air cooling, ventilation, and heating equipment) to make up for what properly designed windows could otherwise do; that is, what is done with an expenditure of expensive energy resources could be done with careful window designs that are in tune with natural processes.

In many parts of the world, techniques for controlling light, air, privacy, and views with windows are highly sophisticated. Some techniques have evolved; their precise origins are unknown and they are usually taken for granted by the people who use them. For instance, there are the traditional shuttered and baffled windows that lend their ubiquitous presence to the texture and character of urbanism throughout the Mediterranean world. They are more complex than they first seem. Usually there are three layers of operable elements. First, there are the shutters which fasten to the outside wall and close across the opening to shade it from the sun or close out the prying eyes of the night, while at the same time permitting breezes to flow freely through. Also, they permit occupants of taller buildings to peer down the street while limiting others from looking in upon them in the cool, shadowed interior of their room. The next elements are a set of glazed casements which might be hinged to open out or to be opened in, depending upon the thickness of the wall in relation to the width of the opening. Finally, there are the solid

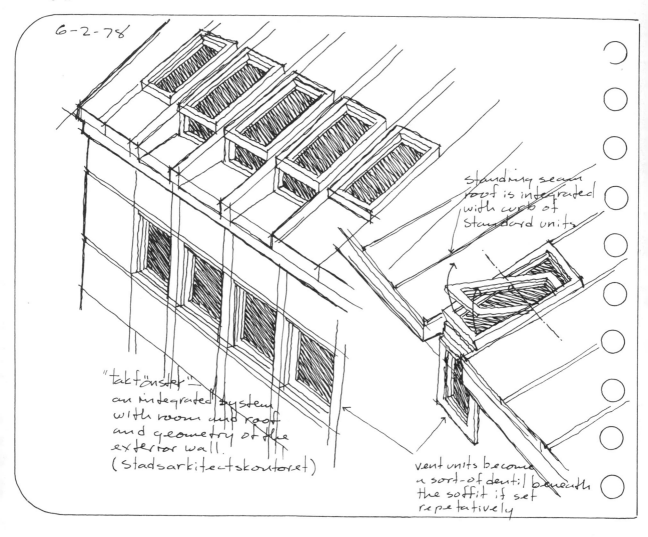

6-2-78

standing seam
roof is integrated
with curb of
standard units

"takfönster"
an integrated system
with room and roof
and geometry of the
exterior wall.
(Stadsarkitectskontoret)

vent units become
a sort-of dentil beneath
the soffit if set
repetatively

paneled interior shutters which are sometimes hinged to the inside wall and sometimes hinged from the window casement leaves themselves. These provide an uncompromising privacy barrier and could (although seldom do) provide a weathertight seal against the cold of winter nights. A facade of these windows registers the mood of the moment within and changes throughout the day. A shuttered wall at midday indicates siesta, glowing slits of lights from the louvers at night might indicate an evening's meal being taken within, or a party going on in the cool hours of the evening, made private from the street but continuing to take advantage of the night's cool breezes.

In quite another climate, Swedes use a modern window which has remarkable talents of its own. Because of a highly refined wood frame, it is as air and water tight on a roof as in a vertical wall. In the north, where light is low and frequently diffused, flexibility in arrangement and in forming combinations of multiple window units is particularly important. The units are usually double or triple glazed, with thin "venetian" type blinds held in one of the spaces between layers of glass so that they never get dusty or rattled by the wind. The blinds can be withdrawn into the head of the window with a crank or a nylon cord and they can be adjusted when they are extended to break the light and view, or close

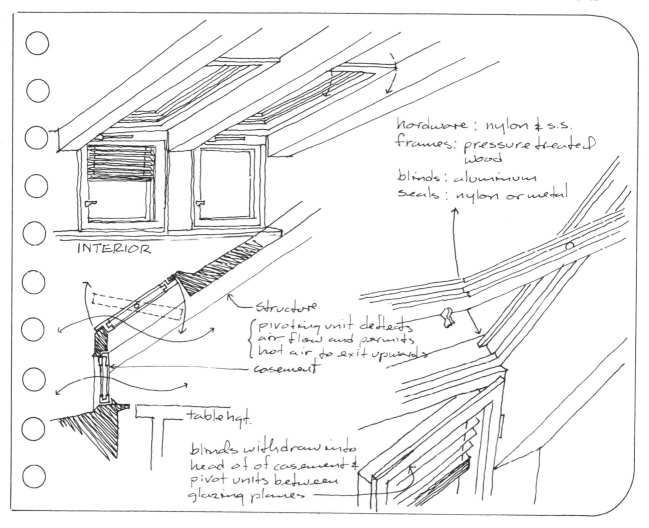

hardware: nylon & s.s.
frames: pressure treated
wood
blinds: aluminum
seals: nylon or metal

INTERIOR

Structure
{ pivoting unit deflects
air flow and permits
{ hot air to exit upwards
casement

table hgt.

blinds withdraw into
head of of casement &
pivot units between
glazing planes

it off entirely. Some of their range of application is indicated by the accompanying notes. Missing from these studies are sectional drawings showing the detailed construction of the windows and how they are installed. These drawings are available, however, in a book of Swedish standards for products used by the construction industry and it would be a waste of time to redraw them in a journal. Instead, photocopies were made from the book of standards and inserted in the notebook.

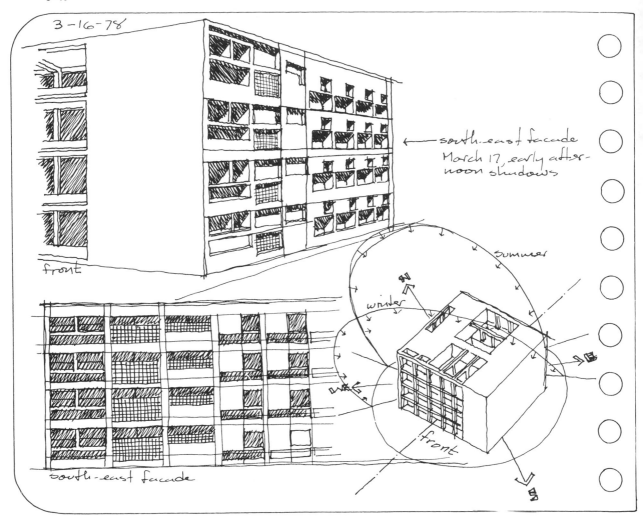

3-16-78

front

← south-east facade March 17, early afternoon shadows

summer

winter

front

south-east facade

Ultimately, there must be a concern for the wall in relation to windows. Shading, screening, privacy, responses to various angles of the sun at different times of year, insulation against the weather, frames to enhance a view from within, and patterns to give expression to a building's exterior are all concerns which can be solved through a careful integration of window and wall. Two buildings which were investigated with respect to solving these problems are a tobacco company's building in Rome and a building formerly called Casa del Fascio, in Como, Italy. In each case, visual notes demonstrate, generally, how they accomplish these tasks.

Casa del Fascio was designed to adjust to its position with respect to natural elements in a comprehensive way. Each facade or elevation is different, depending not only upon what functions and rooms lie behind each exterior wall, but also with respect to subtleties of sun orientation. Each of the four facades is composed of "layers" such that, although made of thin modern materials, the effect is one of considerable depth. This depth-with-layers is

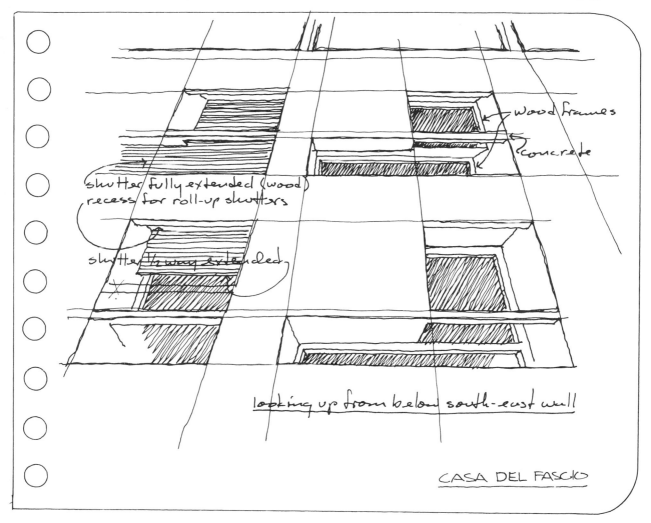

wood frames

concrete

shutter fully extended (wood)
recess for roll-up shutters

shutter ½ way extended

looking up from below south-east wall

CASA DEL FASCIO

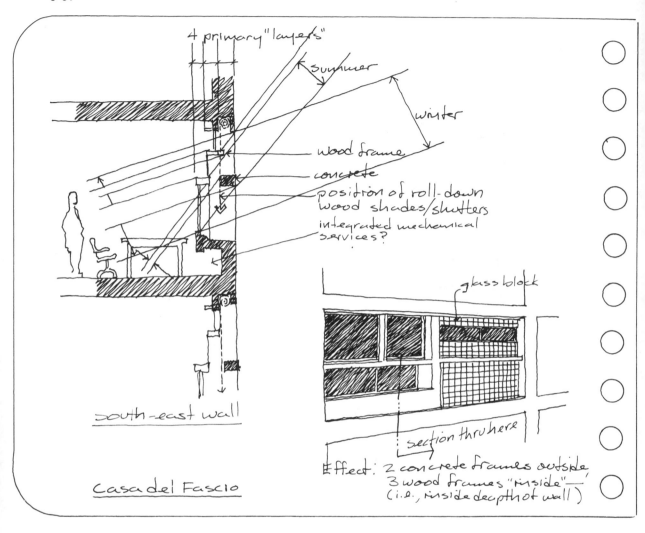

4 primary "layers"

summer

winter

wood frame

concrete

position of roll-down
wood shades/shutters

integrated mechanical
services?

glass block

section thru here

south-east wall

Casa del Fascio

Effect: 2 concrete frames outside
3 wood frames "inside"—
(i.e., inside depth of wall)

best seen in the drawings of a section at an office window, and a view looking up from below. Included here are notes on the southeast wall only. Other walls are similar, though somewhat different in response to interior considerations and sun exposures specific to their particular orientation. The drawings of the wall in question are rather elaborate and time-consuming. They could have been done more easily and with greater accuracy by a camera. However, the act of doing them—laying them out, fitting in the details, adjusting the openings to one another—led to an understanding of them that looking at a photograph a week after the visit could not provide. The act of drawing them generated questions which begged closer, more detailed observations.

For instance: how is the depth of the glazing plane behind the outer surface of the wall related to both winter and summer high sun angles? How are the openings proportioned and arranged to present such harmonious an ensemble across the facade? Section drawings with furniture, sun angles, a scale figure, and a two-dimensional elevation with regulating lines begin to answer these questions. A section through this wall estimates the position of "the layers" and their effect upon direct sunlight entering the rooms. Drawings like this one were done for openings on other walls to explore the architect's response in the design of windows to various orientations and their respective sun angles.

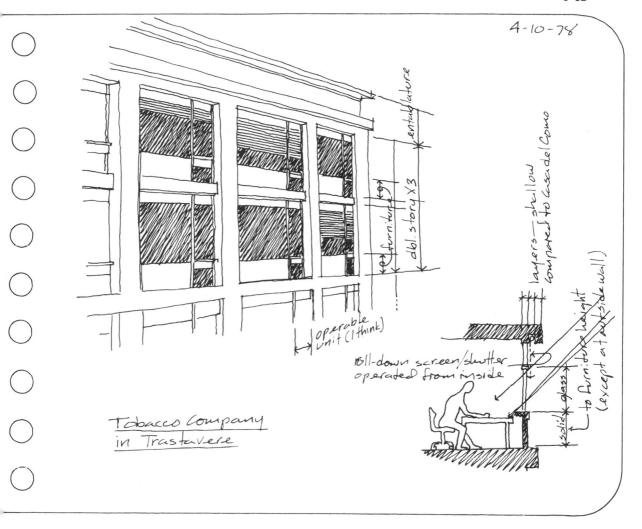

4-10-78

entablature

layers-shallow compared to Casa del Como

dbl. story X3

furniture top

to furniture height
(except at outside wall)

solid glass

operable unit (I think)

Roll-down screen/shutter operated from inside

Tobacco Company
in Trastevere

The tobacco company's building in Rome presents a much more generalized solution to the accommodation of exterior–interior considerations. Each rectangle within the nominal structural frame of the facade is subdivided into constituent functional parts. Although layered, the whole wall is much thinner and there is no accommodation to varying orientations in the basic shape of openings. Adjustments, however, can be made at each window grouping to screen out the sun or admit a cool breeze. The larger of the three glass panels is fixed but the other two appear to be adjustable to admit air. The lower one is screened. A pull-down screen of wood or metal operates from inside and can be stopped at any appropriate position. A strip of opaque material at the top of each grouping "squeezes" the width of the sun shaft entering the interior space to compensate for an inadequate overhead projection in such a shallow facade wall.

The drawings on just one page of the notebook explore these and other features of this window and document them for any possible future reference after memory of specifics has dimmed.

An author keeps a journal to collect his thoughts so that they may be gathered together when the time has come to write. This is practical because the journal assists in the application of his craft. However, the associations which the journal has made help to extend writing beyond craft, helping to give greater substance and insight to what is said. For a designer whose journal is necessarily a visual as well as a written instrument, the situation is the same. If the journal has been fed well enough over a long period of time, it can begin to shape those blurred notions, hunches, and passing observations into ideas of substance, worthy of confidence.

To demonstrate how a journal can contribute to a designer's principal task, we have created an architectural sketch project which is informed by the case studies and notes from pages of the journal. We trust that this sketch project can be seen as analogous to any design project which benefits from its author's experience and incisiveness. Once again there is a story within a story: the detailed explanation of the design is unimportant in itself, except that it is necessary to an understanding of the process by which information recorded from observations may be used to inform a design solution.

The design project is a university complex, the International Center for Visiting Artists and Scholars. Its purpose is to provide living and working facilities for artists and scholars from outside the university and,

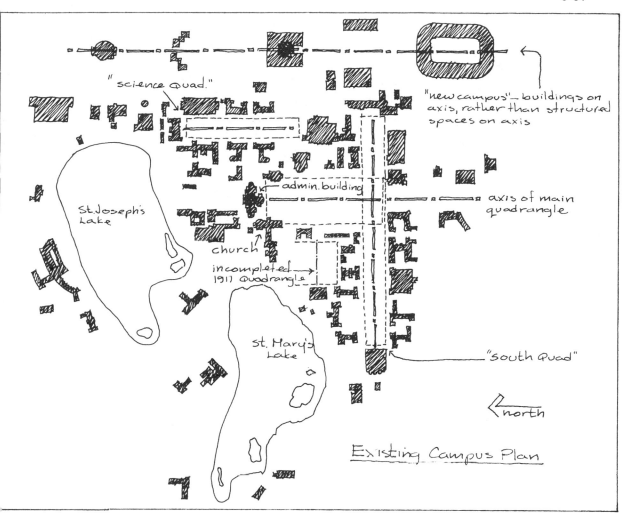

"science Quad."

"new campus"- buildings on
axis, rather than structural
spaces on axis

admin. building

St. Joseph's
Lake

axis of main
quadrangle

church

incompleted
1911 Quadrangle

St. Mary's
Lake

"south Quad"

north

Existing Campus Plan

especially, outside the country. The visitors will spend predetermined lengths of time working with university faculty and students on specific projects and issues of mutual interest. The focus of the program which the Center fosters is basically humanistic and humanitarian.

A first step in a design process such as this involves a study of the project site. The site is on the campus of the University of Notre Dame near South Bend, Indiana. The campus is composed of quadrangles bounded mostly by Victorian Gothic, Victorian Italianate, and Neo-Gothic buildings. One such quadrangle remains incomplete, bounded loosely on three sides and opening onto a view over a lake at one corner. These facing pages show an early aerial

photograph of this part of the campus and a drawing from a similar vantage point showing the basic organization of the campus. This loosely defined quadrangle was selected for the International Center. It was set out in 1917 and intended to be completed with the campus library as the primary focus at one end. The library was built and, now converted to an academic building, remains the only Neo-Renaissance building on the campus.

The overall campus is laid out as a pattern of rectangular open spaces, or quadrangles, based upon a north–south axis which terminates at the University's domed administration building. The result is a simple north–south orthogonal grid for all the campus buildings except the oldest

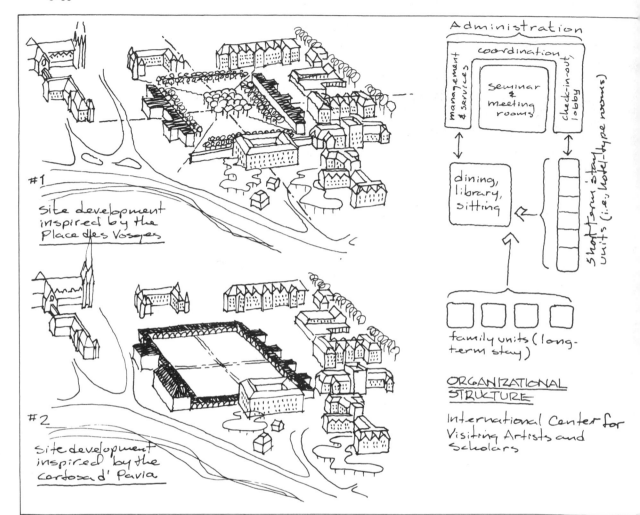

#1

Site development
inspired by the
Place des Vosges

#2

Site development
inspired by the
Certosa d' Pavia

Administration

coordination

management & services

seminar & meeting rooms

check-in-out, lobby

Short-term stay units (i.e., hotel-type rooms)

dining, library, sitting

family units (long-term stay)

ORGANIZATIONAL STRUCTURE

International Center for Visiting Artists and Scholars

ones which are oriented in response to an implied grid generated by the near shoreline of a small lake. The sketch of the campus plan shows the relationship between the two grids. It has been observed that, because the primary grid is so dominant, the venerable old buildings sited with respect to the lake edge now appear to be forgotten and miscellaneous. Therefore at the onset of the design project it was decided that the new project should bring the midnineteenth century buildings into a recognizable relationship with the later ones.

Another site-related decision involved the proposed new building's relationship with the facades of the surrounding buildings. In the belief that the new building should be quietly integrated with the existing buildings, the proportions, rhythms of openings and other characteristics should be compatible with the Neo-Renaissance library and the Victorian style buildings near it.

At the most basic level, the program for the International Center for Visiting Artists and Scholars is simple. It calls for two relatively large buildings and four small ones. The small ones are faculty houses, the largest one is the Center's administrative facility and short-term lodging for visitors, and the intermediate-sized building is to house the dining hall, the kitchen, and the library-sitting room. This latter building is to be rather important for the Center in symbolic

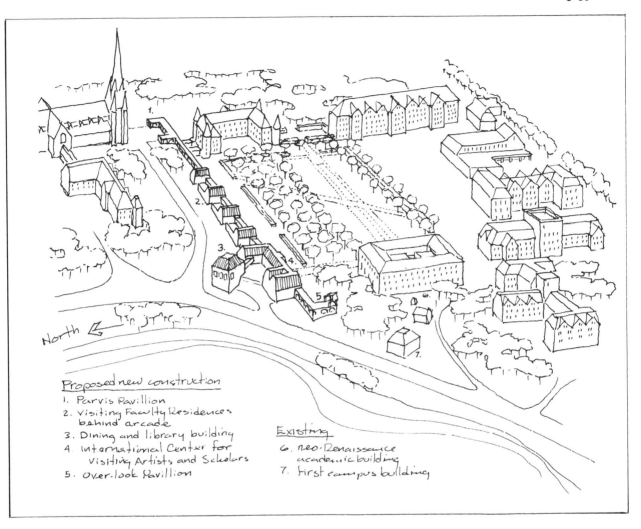

North

Proposed new construction
1. Parvis Pavillion
2. Visiting Faculty Residences behind arcade
3. Dining and library building
4. International Center for Visiting Artists and Scholars
5. Over-look Pavillion

Existing
6. neo-Renaissance academic building
7. First campus building

terms because it houses the primary rooms which bring the visiting scholars together with one another and with the University community.

A decision which is basic to the integration of the proposed facility with the existing campus is that the new buildings should complete the quadrangle, consistent with the 1917 campus plan and the spirit of the University's founder's concept of quadrangles and French axial planning techniques. (The founder and first president Fr. Soren, a priest from LeMans, France, came by way of Canada to found the University in 1842. His penchant for French axial planning is evident throughout the original campus.)

Among the observations in the journal which might inform a design solution for the Center are the Place des Vosges, Addison Court, the University of Virginia, and the Certosa di Pavia. The Place des Vosges suggests a strongly unified space defined by surrounding arcades and reiterated by the landscape pattern. The strong unity it suggests, however, is too complete to permit the variety of entrance and exit conditions and varying visual and functional requirements already in place at or near the periphery. Addison Court encourages a careful integration of the new with the existing and it further suggests a primary and secondary axis as a central organizing feature of the court rather than the equal biaxial situation of the Place des Vosges.

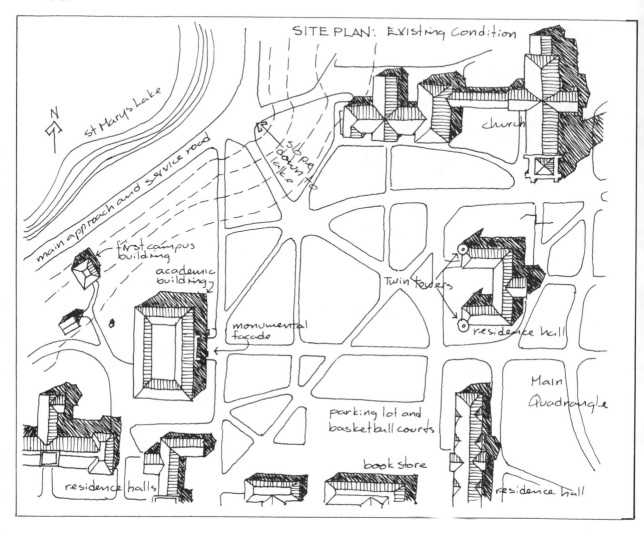

SITE PLAN: EXISTING Condition

N

St Marys Lake

main approach and service road

slope down to lake

church

Twin towers

residence hall

first campus building

academic building

monumental façade

Main Quadrangle

parking lot and basketball courts

book store

residence halls

residence hall

Once again, however, the central space is too unified to suggest a direct analogy for the design solution. The University of Virginia, like Addison Court, suggests a dominant central axis. Further, the axis at Virginia is directional, a situation which, though excessive for our project, is appropriate to the location of the Neo-Renaissance building's position "at the head" of the quadrangle at Notre Dame. Finally, both the University of Virginia and the Certosa di Pavia suggest a solution to the incorporation of the four smaller buildings with the larger ones along a wall, colonnade, or arcade which can give definition to the open side of the quadrangle. The farm complexes in Normandy and Brittany might also inspire a hierarchical arrange-

ment of large public open space in relation to small private outdoor spaces along a wall and in conjunction with smaller buildings.

Urbino suggests that the linear organizing elements for circulation can provide an order based upon connecting one place with another. On the campus, an arcade like that at the Place des Vosges or the Certosa di Pavia could link the church with the lake, two items which figure into the University's history in an important way. (The original name for the school is Université Notre Dame du Lac, referring to the lake beside which the first campus buildings were placed.)

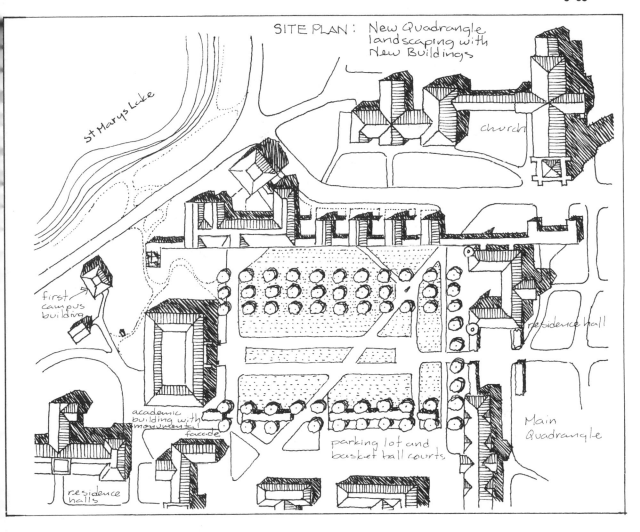

SITE PLAN: New Quadrangle landscaping with New Buildings

St Marys Lake

church

first campus building

residence hall

academic building with monumental facade

parking lot and basket ball courts

Main Quadrangle

residence halls

The ground plan of the proposed solution and the campus as it now exists are compared in the drawings above. The proposal structures the quadrangle by introducing the continuous arcade or colonnade along the north side and "fastening" the other buildings behind it. The dispersal of these buildings along the edge of the open space would not provide the sense of enclosure desired without the incorporation of the continuous arcade which then acts as a datum to the collection of buildings behind it. The arcade helps to lock the new facility into the campus by making it integral with significant elements of on-going campus life, the church and the lake shore. The eastern terminus of the arcade provides a pavilion as a parvis shelter in front of the door of the church to allow the crowds

which gather there after daily masses, weddings, and funerals to congregate under cover when days are hot or the weather is otherwise inhospitable. At the other end of the arcade is a pavilion, providing a platform for over-looking the lake and the picturesque buildings among the trees on the opposite shore. The over-look pavilion also provides a stair for pedestrians to descend from the quadrangle to the lake shore.

The landscaping within the large public quadrangle takes its cues from the Place des Vosges, although the pattern of the ground plan of the quadrangle is not as regular as the Place des Vosges, owing in part to the asymmetrical disposition of the existing buildings. The careful articulation of axes recalls its derivation from a more

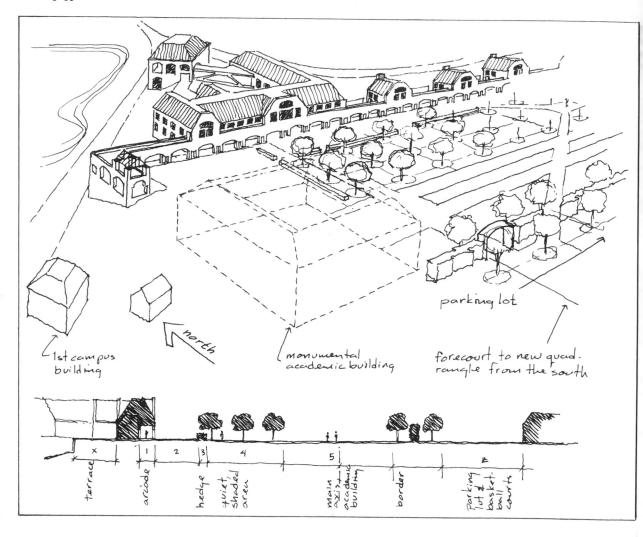

1st campus building

north

monumental academic building

parking lot

forecourt to new quadrangle from the south

terrace | x

arcade | 1

hedge | 2 | 3

quiet, shaded area | 4

main axis / academic building | 5

border

parking lot & basketball courts | z

regular order. This purposeful recollection is consistent with the concept of "potential order" noted from Rudolf Arnheim's American Academy lecture. It can also be seen as analogous to Stockholm's "idealized city plan" where although the actual plan differs considerably from the ideal, it derives its coherence and logic from making reference to the regularized and static order of the ideal.

The Center's main building acts as a gateway to the symbolically important library and dining hall building. These elements extend an axis which begins at the entrace to the main student dining hall located about 250 yards directly south. The student dining hall building is one of Notre Dame's architectural treasures, a large 1920s Collegiate Gothic structure by the Boston architect, Ralph Adams Cram.

The library/dining hall has been freed from the geometry of the quadrangle and is given a somewhat idealized figural shape to distinguish its unique symbolic role. Its orientation relates to the lake edge, rather than the quadrangle so as to imply a reference to issues which extend far

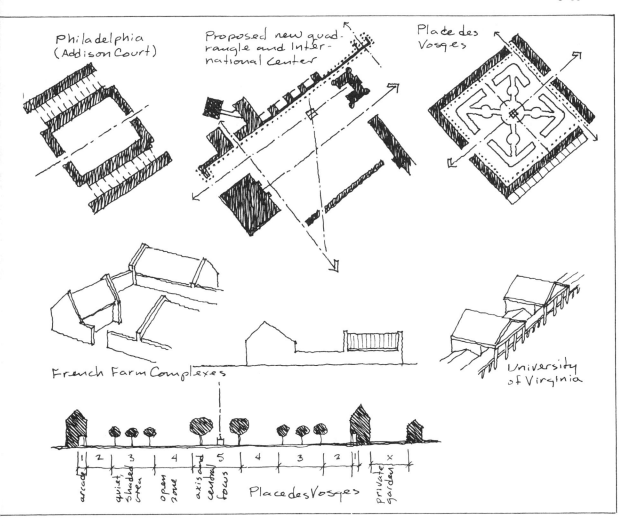

Philadelphia (Addison Court)

Proposed new quadrangle and International Center

Place des Vosges

French Farm Complexes

University of Virginia

1 arcade
2 quiet shaded area
3 open zone
4
5 axis and central focus
Place des Vosges
private garden x

beyond the campus with its rather cloistered community. Further, its form and orientation recall the University's first building located along the same road to the southwest of the proposed Center.

The quadrangle itself is landscaped to help give sense and organization to the activities which surround it. For instance, the new planting along the southern edge screens a parking lot so that the parklike atmosphere of the quadrangle and the dignified quality of the adjoining buildings need not compete with the clutter of cars, asphalt paving, and service access ways. Rows of trees provide roomlike spaces, drawing out some of the spatial qualities of the buildings. Pathways and sidewalks are

reorganized into an uncluttered pattern, and landscaped "vestibules" are developed at significant entrances to the quadrangle, all recalling the landscaped corridors and spaces in the Place des Vosges.

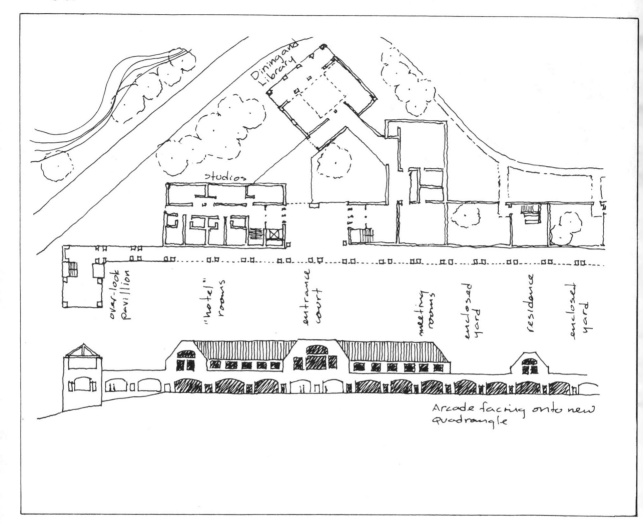

The arcade and the buildings which
become a part of it present a continuous
facade to the quadrangle. A desire for unity
suggested a regular repetitive facade as the
Place des Vosges. However, the irregular
layout of existing buildings on three sides
of the quadrangle requires a balance of
continuous and discontinuous rhythms. The
balance seemed to lay somewhere between
the irregular, individual expressions of the
street facade across from Addison Court in
Philadelphia and the cadence of the new
houses which were so regular as to become
monotonous.

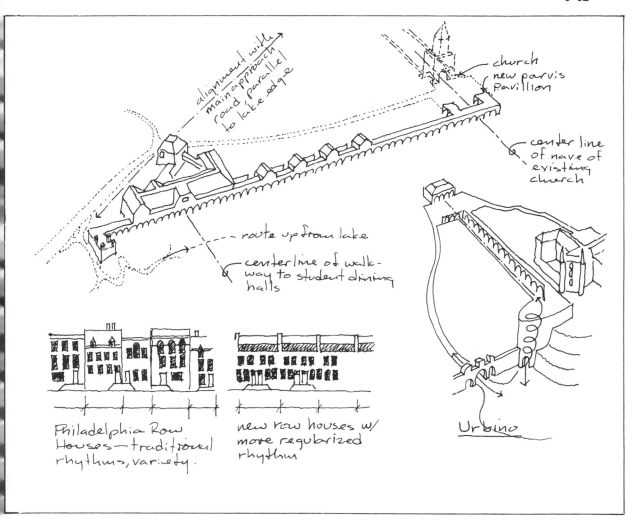

alignment with main approach road, parallel to lake edge

church
new parvis
Pavillion

center line of nave of existing church

route up from lake

center line of walk-way to student dining halls

Philadelphia Row Houses—traditional rhythms, variety.

new row houses w/ more regularized rhythm

Urbino

An implicit assumption in designing the Center was that it must complement and reinforce what are virtues of the existing environment. The basic strategy was to consider the campus to be incomplete and the designer's task to achieve completion. Therefore, the arcade completes the quadrangle and connects two important, related "pieces" of the campus: the church and the lake shore. The strategy of seeing the site as wanting completion presumes a "sense of place" or *genius loci* to which the designer must become sensitive before embarking on any modifications, lest he destroy the unique and subtle qualities of the place.

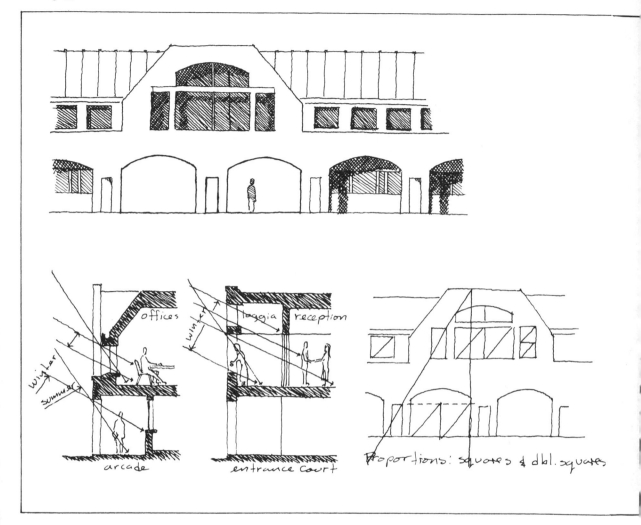

The long south-facing facade of the Center provided an excellent opportunity to create openings which contribute to the interplay of rhythms of buildings and repetitive arches, and which control the penetration of sunlight to provide cooling shade in the summer and deep direct sun penetration in the winter. Assisting the design of these windows was the study of windows recorded earlier. The window designs benefitted in a more detailed way than shown here, including means for controlling air circulation, framing special views, and dealing with the diffuse north light while mitigating the severity of prevailing winter winds from the north and west.

Finally, the Castelvecchio notes informed the solution with respect to the simultaneous requirement for joining and separating the library/dining hall and the Center's main building. The "connection" at Castelvecchio joined diverse parts of the ruin and the modern construction with fragments of historical background associated with the castle. It did so by generating a collage of disparate elements which would then mingle at this significant juncture of the museum complex. In the International Center project, the library/dining hall building is set askew of the primary orthogonal geometry to separate it and give it its objectlike and idealized quality. It is then rejoined to the Center by a bridge and a terrace extended from the main entrance

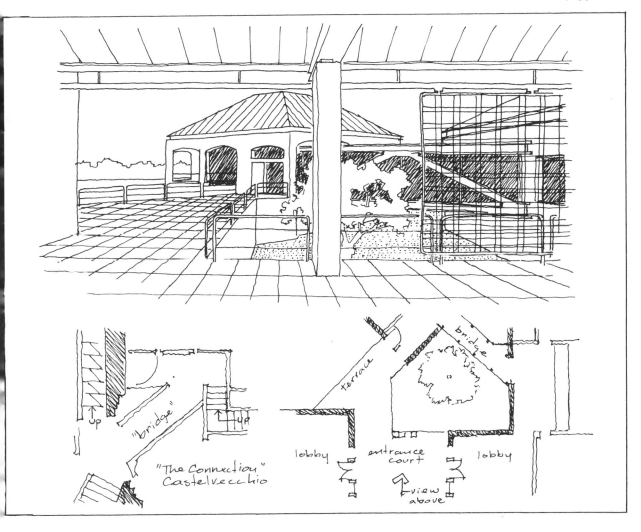

court. The library/dining hall building is seen through the entrance portal to the Center, framed by an opening which is derived from the geometry that is consistent with the entire quadrangle. Abrupt changes in levels, parts of buildings which seem to overlap, portions of each building seen through grills, and overlapping handrails recall the visual collage of the "connection" at Castelvecchio.

This project for an International Center involved many more design considerations than those noted here. For instance, we have shown none of the interiors and have not related any of the technological decisions which must be made. Many of the design decisions are recounted only in part; for example, the basic proportions, style,

and character of the new building has much to do with the proportions, style, and character of existing buildings but we do not illustrate that in detail here.

The project we have shown is largely hypothetical; its purpose is to provide an example of the tie between thought and action through use of a journal. Memories fade. What seemed to be good ideas at the time are often overlooked because there is no application in sight. A journal can preserve those thoughts and images and bring them together so that patterns emerge, associations form, and when unforseen circumstances arise, they may be informed by thoughts and observations recorded before in the journal.

A Collection of Visual Notes

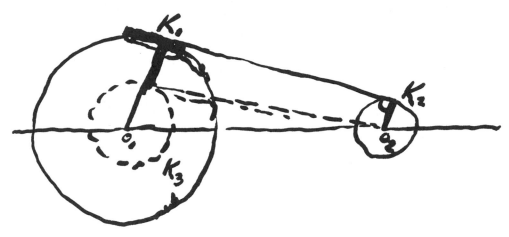

4-1 Based on a sketch by Albert Einstein.

We have assembled this book in the belief that visual note-taking is a skill which can and should be developed by architects and designers. In the previous chapter we showed how one architect used visual notes to record, analyze, and design. In this chapter we hope to further convince you by presenting several different examples of visual note-taking by design professionals. We have also gathered examples of visual notes from people in a diverse range of other professions. These examples not only stretch our conceptions of the possibilities in visual notation but also act as precursors of the development of visualization as a skill appropriate to any endeavor and a major support for creativity.

THINKING AND CREATIVITY

It is quite common to accept thinking as comprised of a set of rational skills which can be measured and for which we can set norms for development. These skills are tested through the media by which institutional education seeks to develop thinking, namely, reading, writing, and arithmetic and their derivatives. The thinking capabilities for which reliable, quantifiable educational vehicles have not been developed tend to be defined outside the realm of "basic" thinking and are lumped under headings such as intuition or talent. As a result of this narrow definition of thinking, a number

of mental skills are left undeveloped by a "basic" education.

Research into the functions of the brain have identified two major categories of thinking characteristics:[11]

verbal	nonverbal
analytic	synthetic
symbolic	concrete
abstract	analogic
temporal	nontemporal
rational	nonrational
digital	spatial
logical	intuitive
linear	holistic

Both sets of functions are necessary to thinking and skills should be developed which utilize each of these functions. With this understanding, the definition of thinking is expanded as is the definition of basic education.

The other way in which we have limited our understanding of thinking has been through the confusion of thinking with brain capacity. While brain size in humans has changed very little through recorded history, thinking ability has evolved in response to evolving culture and changing contexts. This is further complicated by our attraction to the dramatic or heroic. In tribal cultures, a person who could relieve pain was considered to have magic powers and held a position

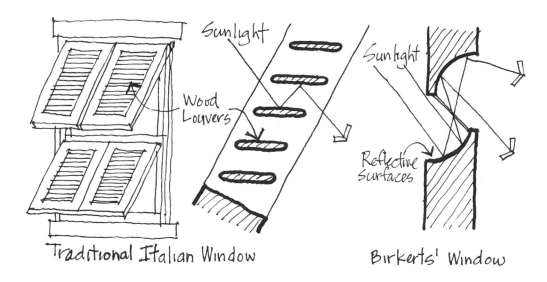

Sunlight

Wood Louvers

Sunlight

Reflective Surfaces

Traditional Italian Window

Birkerts' Window

4-2A Analogous solutions: shutter and window design by Gunnar Birkerts.

of great power in his village. In the Middle Ages, Europeans who had learned mathematics from Arab sources were considered to be geniuses and were often among the most important advisors to the king. Many of those feats which were so rare in the past are routinely performed by children in primary school today. They are considered to be part of basic education.

Changing contexts evoke new needs for thinking and constantly expand the realm of normal thinking ability. Until now, creativity, invention, and intuition have been considered extraordinary skills, available only to the gifted. But the contexts for thinking are changing dramatically. We live in a highly complex world with incredible access to information. The farmer, separated by miles from the next family, has become the urban dweller, separated from his neighbor by the thickness of a party wall. Along with the consumer and equal rights movements, each of us has taken on a broad set of concerns and responsibilities. We have begun to realize that a representative form of government rests its success upon an informed and involved citizenry. But we have also found that each problem cannot be solved in isolation. Solutions to educational or environmental problems affect economic, labor, health, and diplomatic problems.

Books, photographs, motion pictures, and now television and computers have changed our world of experience both by virtue of the information they have delivered

and by the speed with which they deliver that information. Without leaving our homes, we have access to a description of the evolution of life on earth, a ballet or play from New York or Moscow, a soccer match in Brazil or a tennis match in France, a view of the ocean depths, and a computer-constructed television picture of Jupiter and Saturn. We can carry a symphony or opera in our pocket while jogging through woods or cycling through cornfields. We are standing in a shower of experiences and information.

These communication media have given us a banquet for thought but each in its own way has changed the manner in which we think. They have changed our image of the world and our image of ourselves—foundations of thought. As with all technology, communication media may be used to the advantage or disadvantage of man and the world in which he lives. They have the capability to entertain and divert, to help us to avoid problems or challenges. They can also be used to understand our world and its problems. In this world, creativity can no longer be the province of a few persons but must become a part of normal thinking. While each of us must exercise our own judgment about the value and propriety of what we create, we need the speed of intuition and the insights of highly developed visual perception to create the harmonies in life that we find in music. Perhaps if we develop "artistic" thinking as a complement of "rational" thinking, coping with the discordance and contradictions of our modern world will be easier.

Wood Cell structure

Sears Tower structure - joined tubes

4-2B   Tree cells and the Sears Tower.

VISUAL NOTE-TAKING

We believe that visualization is conducive to effective thinking; visual literacy is conducive to effective communication; and the practice of keeping visual notes is instrumental in developing both visualization and visual literacy. We have already reviewed the basic functions of visual notetaking: recording, analysis, and design. Here we will look at their contributions to visualization, visual literacy, and creative thinking.

"In drawing you will delve deeply into a part of your mind too often obscured by endless details of daily life. From this experience, you will develop your ability to perceive things freshly in their totality, to see their underlying patterns and possibilities for new combinations. Creative solutions to problems, whether personal or professional, will be accessible through new modes of thinking and new ways of using the power of your whole brain."[12] The key to developing visual thinking and visual perception is to begin to look intensely at the world and its parts on a regular basis. Representative drawing forces us to look. Analytical drawing helps us to abstract structures and generalizations from what we see, reveals order and meaning, and provides visual symbols for complex realities. In design, invention has been defined as the skill of seeing analogies between different problems or needs and analogies between solutions to problems. The architect Gunnar Birkerts saw the problems solved by Italian wooden shutters to be similar to the problems confronting the curtain walls of tall buildings, namely, the admittance of light while excluding heat. Or the structure of the Sears Tower in Chicago can be seen as analogous to the cellular structure of a tree. In each case the image of one object had to be stored in memory and the other object had to be so scrutinized as to perceive the analogies. Equally important, the ability to see analogies comes through _practice_. You must constantly use a skill if it is to be reliable at a given moment or circumstance.

EXAMPLES

In gathering these examples of visual notes and interviewing the people who made them, we noticed some patterns and some peculiarities. All authors held intense, immediate associations with their sketches; they could readily recall the circumstances in which the sketches were made and were usually stimulated to further conversation related to the drawings or their subjects. Most saw their notes not as products but as experiences. They valued these experiences as forms of distraction, entertainment, fantasy, or meditation. Many noted the feeling of relaxation which sketching provided. In just about every case a wide variety of drawing conventions were used; on the same page one will find an aerial view of a city, a perspective of a roof detail, a section through a building, and a diagram of symbolic relationships. Conventions seemed to be adopted spontaneously in reaction to the subject or ideas at hand.

The distinctions between the examples from different note-takers were also significant. Some approached their sketches with a strong focus or sense of purpose, while others regularly sketched with no predetermined intent as if casting a net for fish or wandering in the space of their minds and their perceptions. For some, sketching is integral with their work, while for others it is an escape. There is a wide range of drawing skill exhibited including the incredibly fine detail of the sketches by Laurence Booth and the animated doodles of Leonard Duhl. Each in its own way is very powerful and closely adapted to the temperament and thinking of the individual. The range of occasions for note-taking is very broad as well: visits to towns, buildings, museums, gardens, hardware stores, or book stores; plane rides, train rides, and boat rides; lectures, films, television; client meetings, site analysis, team design meetings, program analysis, schematic design, detailing, building research.

Materials were selected for this chapter with the intent of showing the wide range of subjects, styles, and attitudes we found. For each person, the examples represent only a small portion of his or her work as we were seeking distinctions and extremes rather than a comprehensive view of the visual notes of each person. Nor did we quote the full comments of each author. We found several shared techniques and attitudes toward note-taking among the contributors to this chapter. In meeting the focused objectives of this book we hope we have not done them a disservice and that we will have an opportunity to describe the full richness of their work following more extensive research.

Connotation/Style

In addition to the three major functions of note-taking—recording, analysis, and design—there is an important fourth function: connotation. This is a form of communication which is the product of the manner or style with which the notes are made. The range of styles shown in this chapter reveals the intensely personal nature of the thoughts they convey, emotions ranging from high excitement to calm contemplation, and preferences for precision or informality. Style forms a message to others about our intentions, interests, and motivations. More importantly, style can become a positive reinforcement to note-taking. Style is often like putting on a favorite comfortable sweater, preparing you for relaxed concentration and creative thinking. "Drawing can reveal much about you to yourself, some facets of *you* that might be obscured by your verbal self. Your drawings can show you how to *see* things and how to feel about things."[13] A close look at Alvar Aalto's sketches show this potential. We can imagine him slowly retracing forms and shifting to a calm, attentive state of mind which formed the setting for his powerful insights and inventions.

4-3 Design sketch by Alvar Aalto.

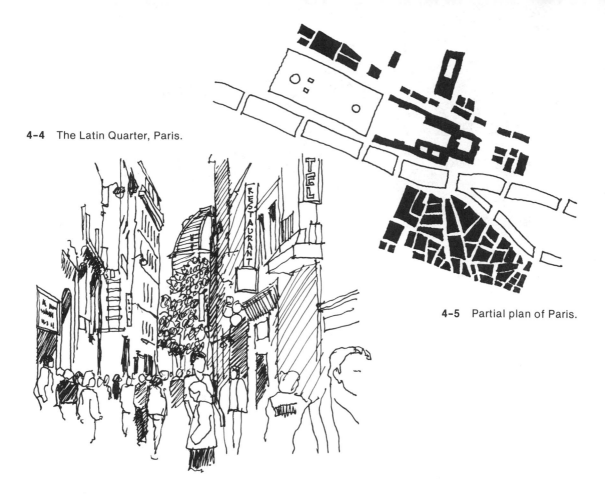

4-4 The Latin Quarter, Paris.

4-5 Partial plan of Paris.

Perception/Conception: a Duality

Another way to view the examples in this chapter is with respect to their degree of abstraction. To the extent that sketches are not actually the realities which they represent, they can all be said to be abstractions. However, there is a wide variance of abstraction between the representation of the direct concrete experience of a restaurant space and the symbol for a restaurant. Because we are all capable of direct perceptions and more abstract conceptions built upon perceptions, our experiences of the world have both perceptual and conceptual content which should be conveyed in our visual notes. If I stroll along a street in the Latin Quarter of Paris,

I have the direct experience of the color and smells of the food stands and the sense of tight enclosure of the buildings which form the street space. The other important part of my experience derives from my knowing where the Latin Quarter sits in a map of Paris and that just a few short blocks away is the River Seine, across which lies an environment of gardens and museums with broad vistas, very different from where I am.

Thus my perceptual experience is heightened by my conceptual experience. Perceptions and conceptions are not in opposition but represent two ends of a spectrum of total experience. They reinforce each other.

Communication

Our last reflections on the visual notes in this chapter concern our encounters with some reluctance to share visual notes. There are many understandable reasons why people are not comfortable with sharing their notes: the notes may be very personal or introspective; they may be considered to be of no importance to someone else or not to be of sufficient quality. As with other things, we may be more willing to share our notes with some people than with others. Each person must judge for himself, but might consider the positive aspects of sharing notes to some degree. In order to pursue our professions and our lives we must constantly communicate with other people. In communicating with these people we are not just passing on information, but sharing an understanding of the meaning of the information. In order to do this successfully, we must share thoughts and attitudes in an informal and more general way. This is why many meetings between architects and their clients often begin with a short period of loose conversation about sports, weather, or current events. They are sharing a common reference as to how they feel at that moment, whether they are pressed for time, or their expectations for the meeting. They are also establishing a level of mutual respect necessary to any discussion of substance.

Visual communication requires the sharing of a similar understanding among people. Informal visual notes often have just the right quality to do this job. Like a good informal conversation, they convey an openness and expectancy not found in formal presentations. These notes can help others understand how one thinks visually and they have the added capability of being able to be read rapidly and comprehensively. They also invite response and further conversation. Many of the values which note-taking holds for the individual can be shared with others to the benefit of all. Perhaps one of the ways to be more effective and creative in addressing problems is to balance individual possession of ideas with free exchanges which produce shared creativity.

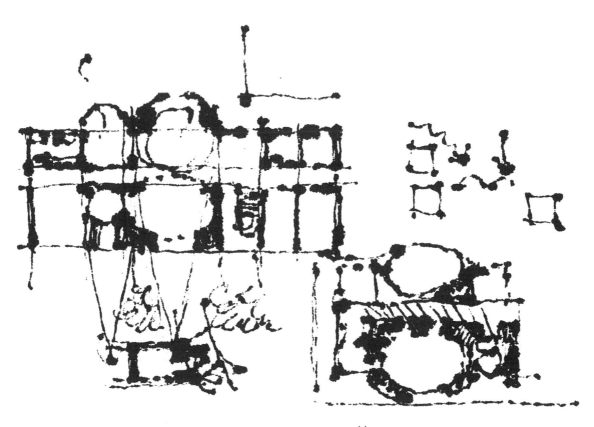

4-6 Sketches on a paper napkin.

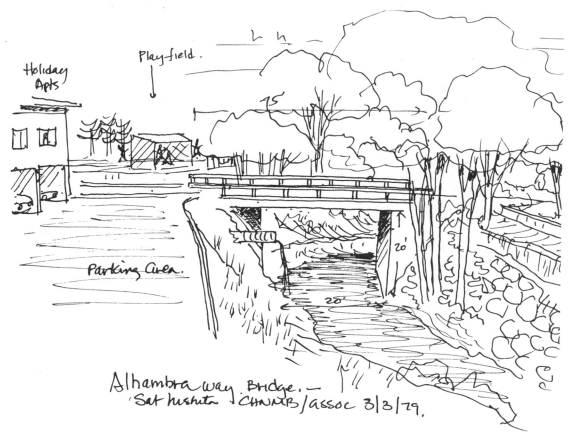

Holiday Apts

Playfield.

Parking Area.

20'

20'

75

20'

Alhambra Way Bridge. —
'Sat Nishita • CHNMB/assoc 3/3/79.

4-7 Site studies.

SATORU NISHITA
Landscape Architect

In keeping with the earlier descriptions of note-taking processes we have organized these examples under the three major headings of recording, analysis, and design. This first example, however, illustrates the degree of integration of note-taking processes often found among creative designers. In this example you will see carefully illustrated observations, exploratory diagrams, and specific design proposals freely mixed in a spontaneous response to the context and design program.

"Sketches 'reflect' and record initial 'impressions' and 'thoughts' about the existing site, the environment and the regional character. They provide a clue as to the importance of the existing major elements, character, and natural surroundings (i.e., vegetation, land forms, hydrology, and urban forms, etc.) which reflect the setting and the context for the proposed project. They also unveil critical problems, issues, constraints, and opportunities through the process of visual observation, graphic notes, and analyses.

"I find them a valuable tool to communicate thoughts and ideas to other members of the team and to stimulate other ideas and discussion by means of feedback from them."

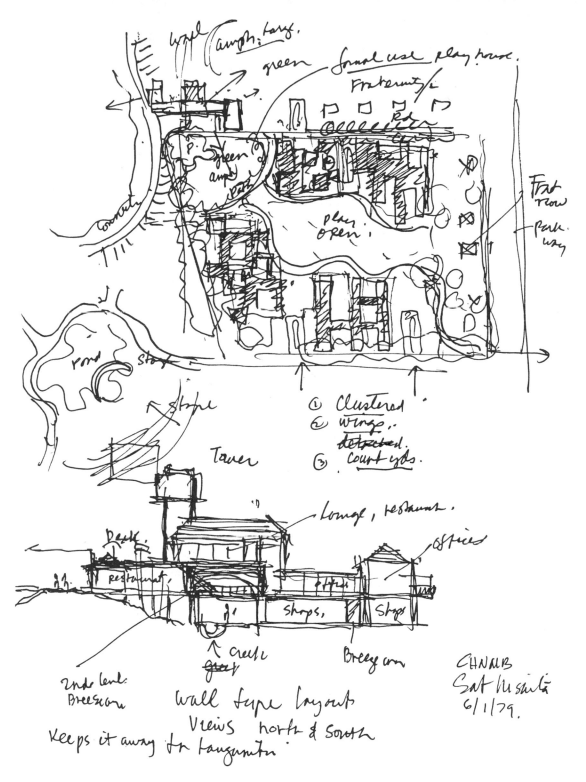

4-8 Site studies.

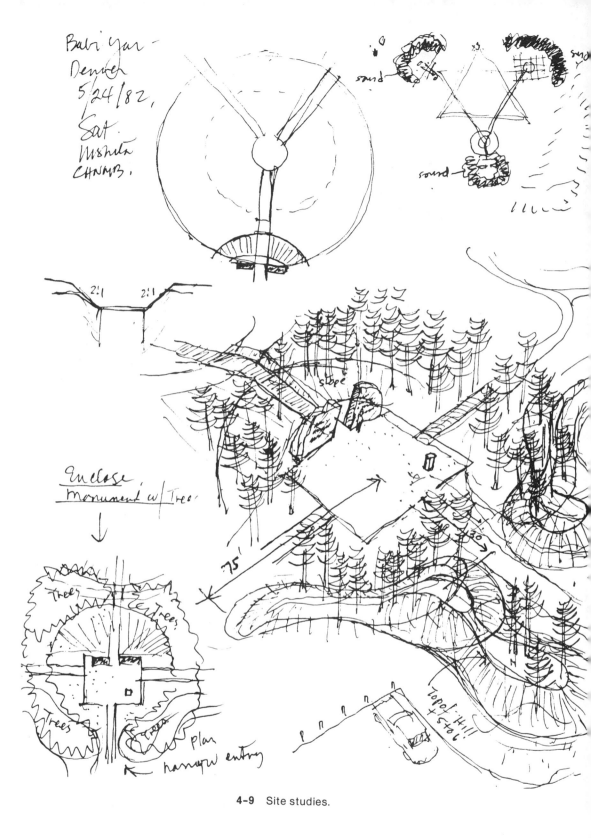

Babi Yar -
Denver
5/24/82,
Sat.
Mishula
CHNMB.

2:1   2:1

Enclose,
monument w/ Trees

Trees

Trees   Trees

plan
narrow entry

slope

75'

30

topof Hill
+ stoi.

4-9 Site studies.

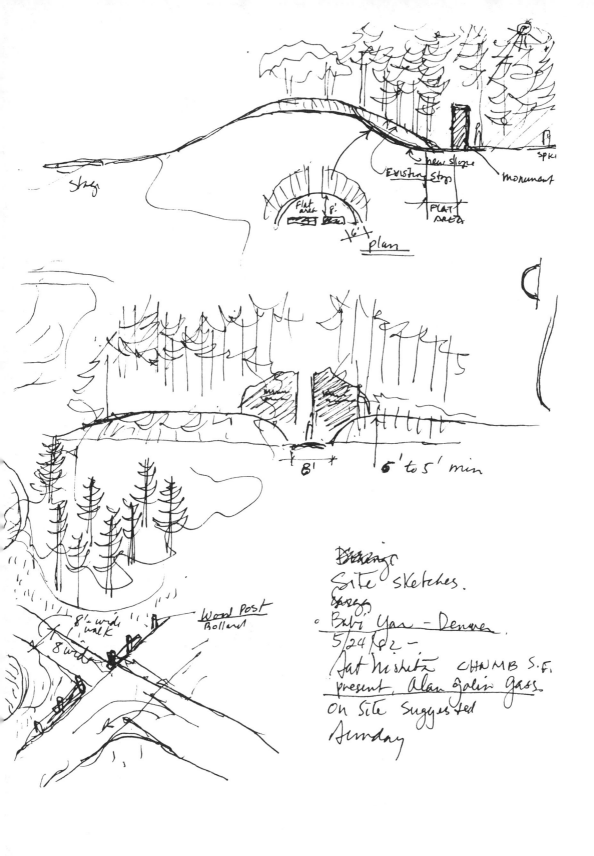

stage

new slope

Existing stop

monument

SPK

Flat area 8'

PLAT AREA

16' plan

8'

6' to 5' min

8'½ wide walk

8' wide

Wood Post Bollard

Site sketches.

Baby Yar - Denver.
5/24/82 -
Jat Nishita CHNMB S.F.
present, Alan Golin gass
On Site Suggested
Sunday

4-10 View of Japanese farms from an airplane.

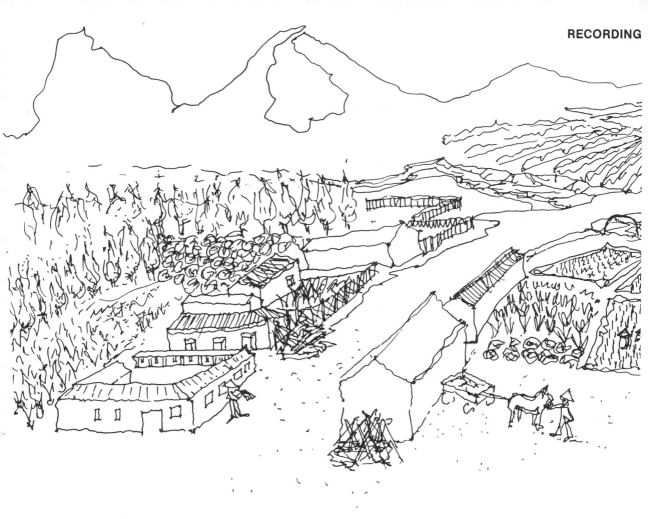

4-11 Countryside in Jilling Province, China.

KATHLEEN M. O'MEARA
Architect

An accomplished recorder of visual information is like a good listener; practice has refined the skills of receptivity to experience. This first example clearly reveals the potential for discovery of an attentive note-taker who is unburdened by preconceptions about her subject.

"Sketching is a skill of the hand that becomes a tool of the mind. To document a space, the process of sketching is a way to see order. In seeing a place a certain image may generate many sketches. As the sketches stray from reality they become ideas. To think in images is to generate a dialogue: sketches as a source of ideas, sketches as a record of thoughts. Sketching is thinking with a pencil."

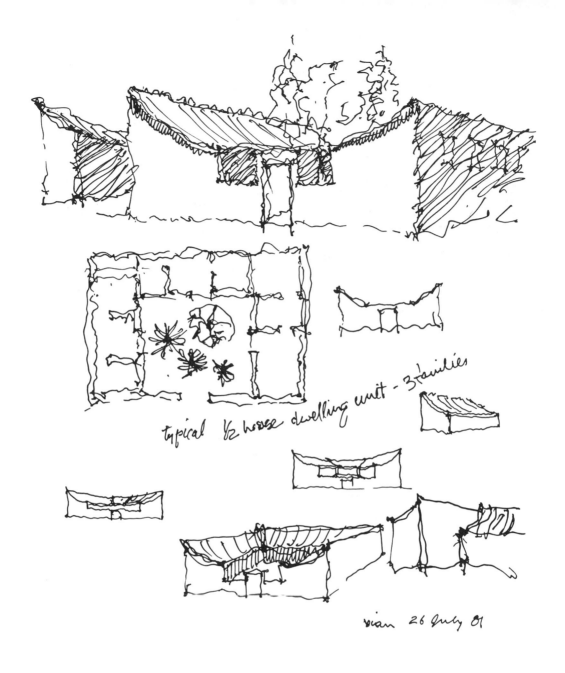

typical ½ house dwelling unit - 3 families

xian 26 July 01

4-12 Half houses of Xian, China.

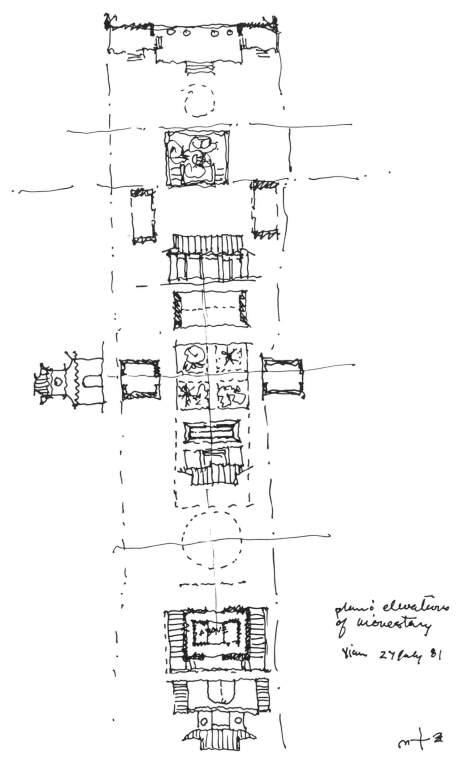

plans elevations
of monestary

Yian 27 July 81

4-13 Monestary at Xian, China.

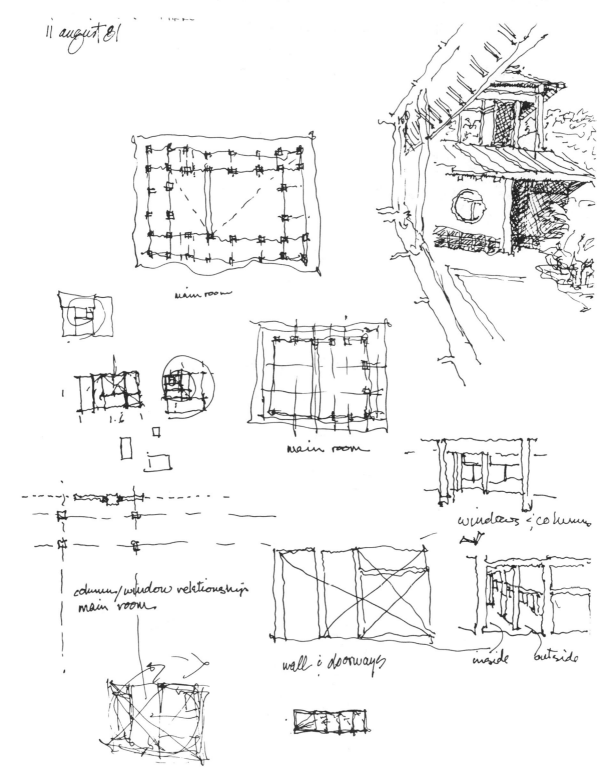

11 august 81

main room

main room

windows & columns

column/window relationship
main room

wall & doorways

inside   outside

4-14 Imperial Villa near Nikko, Japan.

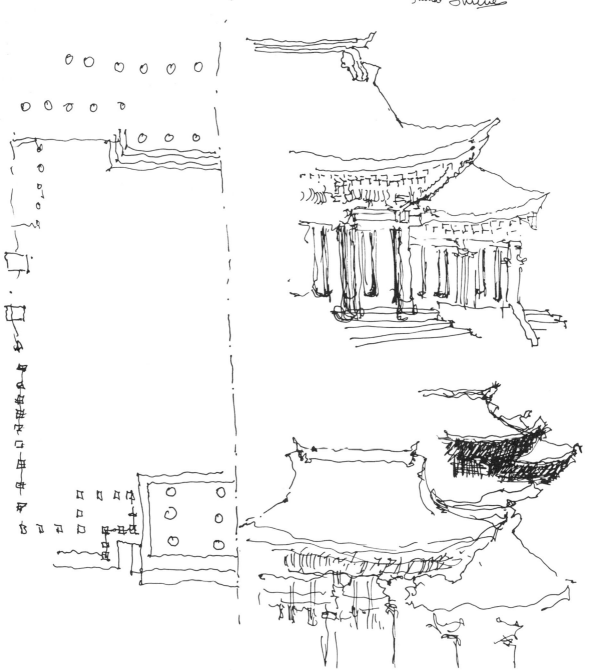

4-15 Shintu shrine-Tokyo.

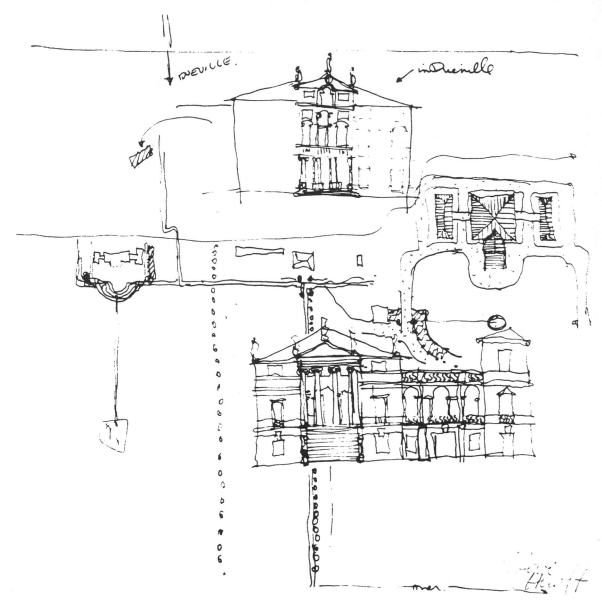

4-16 The Villa Monza at Dueville, Italy.

STEVEN HURTT
Architect

"Drawing reveals relationships that would otherwise escape the eye and hence the mind. These drawings reveal my interest in the farmer's sensitivity to the landscape. The Veneto is thought of as a habitable garden in which fields and buildings ennoble each other."

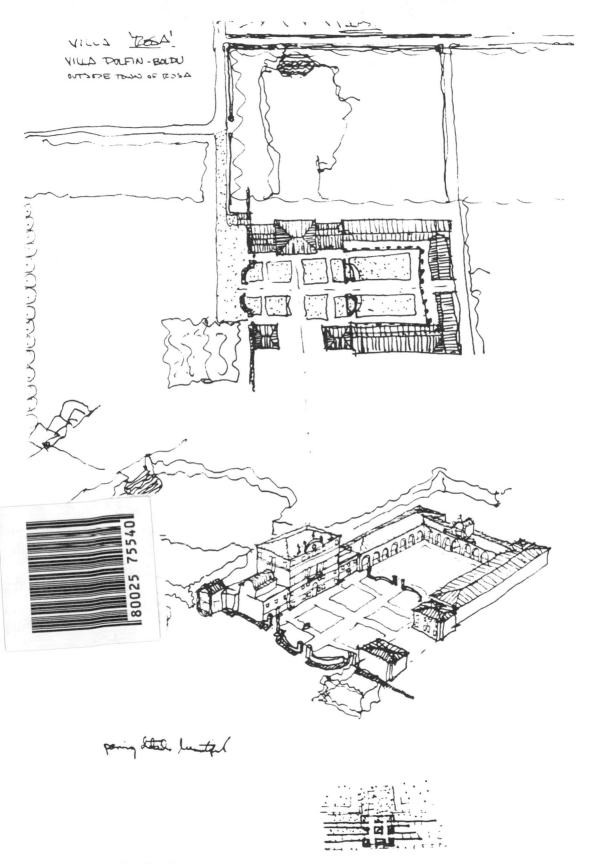

4-17 The Villa ca' Dolfin Boldue near Rosa in the Veneto region of Italy.

THE PONT NEUF

The Pont Neuf connects the Left & Right Banks of Paris with the Ile de la Cité. Walking over the bridge actually gives very little sensation of walking across water — the walls are solid and relatively high this serves as a link between the 3 pieces of land,... almost a denial of the river

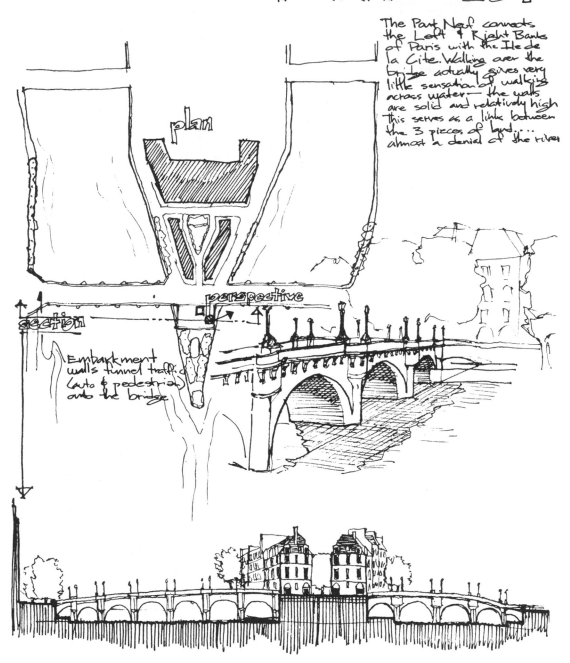

plan

perspective

section

Embankment walls tunnel traffic (auto & pedestrian) onto the bridge

4-18 The Pont Neuf-Paris.

4-19 The Pazzi Chapel-Florence, Italy.

PAUL GATES
Architect

"I find that sketching pushes me to a
higher level of understanding of the built
environment. Through drawing I force
myself beyond rudimentary impressions of
the subject to a keener awareness of the
specific pieces involved in the composition.
Once I have sketched a particular architectural event, a plan detail for instance, and
through the drawing come to understand
how the piece works, by itself and within its
context, that detail then becomes mine, to
implement and modify in the design process as the need arises."

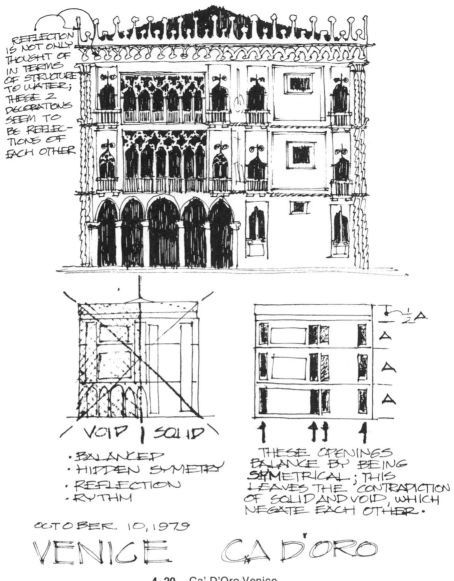

REFLECTION IS NOT ONLY THOUGHT OF IN TERMS OF STRUCTURE TO WATER; THESE 2 DECORATIONS SEEM TO BE REFLECTIONS OF EACH OTHER

VOID | SOLID
· BALANCED
· HIDDEN SYMETRY
· REFLECTION
· RYTHM

THESE OPENINGS BALANCE BY BEING SYMETRICAL; THIS LEAVES THE CONTRADICTION OF SOLID AND VOID, WHICH NEGATE EACH OTHER.

OCTOBER 10, 1979

VENICE   CA D'ORO

4-20   Ca' D'Oro-Venice.

DOUGLAS GAROFALO
Architect

"The obvious aesthetic pleasures aside, drawing provides me with many insights. Physical aspects such as form, texture, and color are easily revealed, as are more abstract qualities regarding design or composition. If I am able to transpose three-dimensional objects or space in the form of a two-dimensional drawing, inherently, I learn. Drawing then, helps me understand what it is I see. Sketching is a tool just as the ability to read is a tool. It is fascinating to realize that such tools are so closely related to aesthetics."

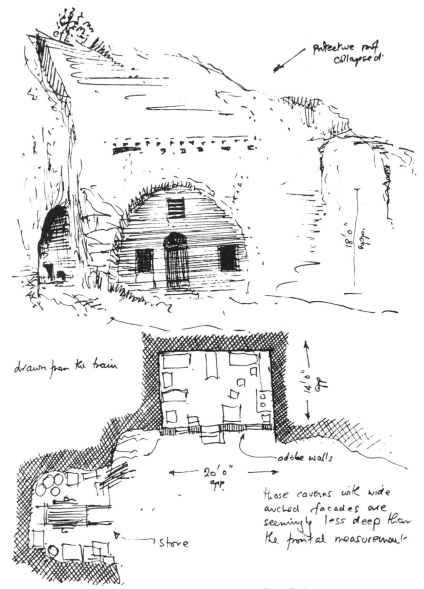

Annotations on drawing:
- architecture roof collapsed.
- drawn from the train
- 18' 0" app.
- 14' 0" app
- adobe walls
- 20' 0" app.
- Store
- those caverns with wide arched facades are seemingly less deep than the frontal measurement

4-21 Pit-court dwellings-Zhong Tau, China.

PATRICK HORSBRUGH
Architect

"In response to the excitement of sketching from life, three compelling influences emerge which intensify the experience. The sense of time past is omnipresent in the form and condition of the subject, involving the artist in the nature of the materials; there is the emotional stimulation of capturing the effect by creative effort; and there is the curiosity that is aroused.

"Whatever the scene, it is 'alive' for me, in the sense that music is alive with previous sounds and subsequent effects yet unheard. This momentary experience is essentially conversational as in a concerto with oneself as the solo response (however inadequate), always in position of inquisitor in expectation.

"Visual impressions represent, for the designer, that essential order of plan and relative disposition, upon which practical application depends, where the spaces between are as important as the objects seen. Here the fascination of these pit-court dwellings of the village of Zhong Tau, near Xi'an, Honan, China, arises as much from the logic of their excavation as from the seclusion and dis-community."

121

4-22 Westdean, England.

BARRY RUSSELL
Architect

This note-taker provides a compelling affirmation of the personal rewards of frequent sketching and recording of observations.

"Most of the sketches included here were done very quickly, many on a brief stop during a walk with whatever implement I have to hand. I carry a sketchbook most of the time and like to sketch whatever I can whilst traveling, walking, or just waiting around. I don't like to go too long without drawing and I have done so ever since I was at school.

"Many sketches become the basis for larger drawings or paintings but that has not happened to any included here. Apart from keeping one in practice, having a sketchbook to help recall an idea, a place, a day, or a feeling is important to me. Some drawings are just explorations of some visual idea, as with the folded facade and these also offer one feedback in relation to buildings, spaces, and landscape."

4-23 Folded facade study.

4-24 Countryside near Goreme, Turkey.

4-25 Older Mill-Sussex, England.

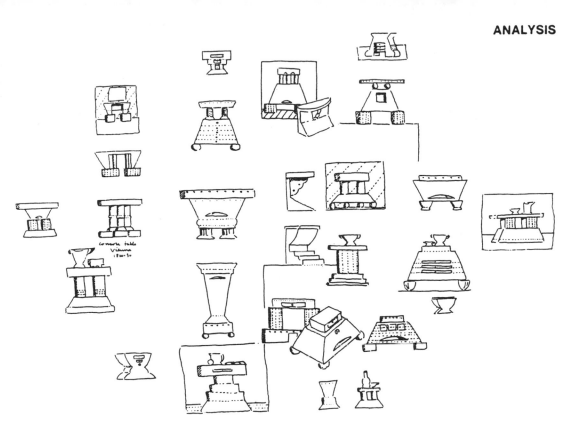

4-26 Table design studies.

MICHAEL GRAVES
Architect

"This type of drawing (preparatory study) documents the process of inquiry, examining questions raised by a given intention in a manner which provides a basis for the later, more definitive work. These drawings are by nature deliberately experimental. They produce variations on themes, and are clearly exercises toward more concrete architectural ends. As such they are generally developed in a series, a process which is not wholly linear but which involves the reexamination of given questions.

"Generally didactic in nature, these studies instruct as much by what is left out as by what is drawn. The manner in which they are able to test ideas and provide the foundation for subsequent development involves a method of leaving questions open through the presumption of incompleteness. . ."[14]

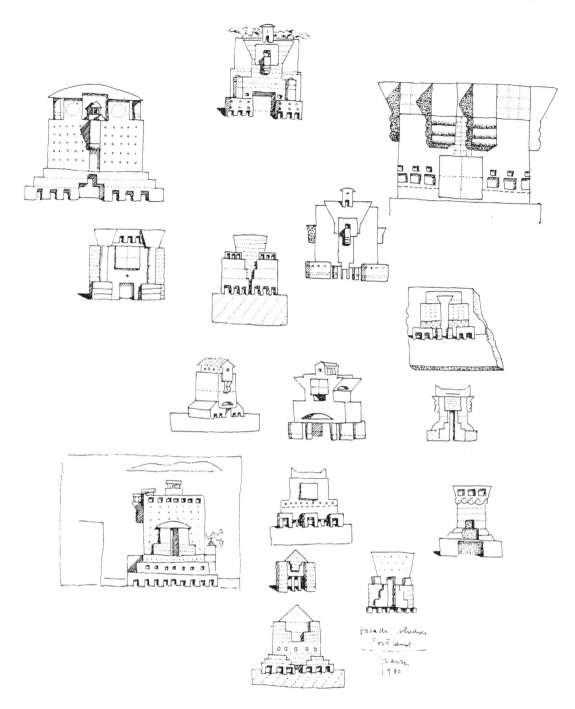

4-27 Facade studies of the Portland Building.

126

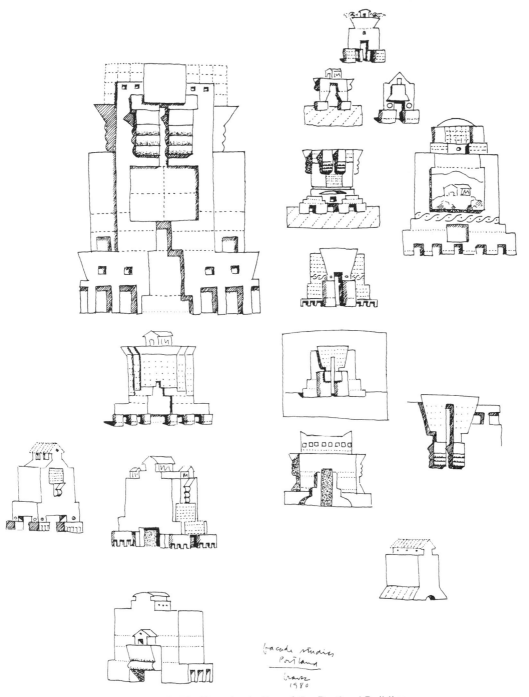

4-28 Facade studies of the Portland Building.

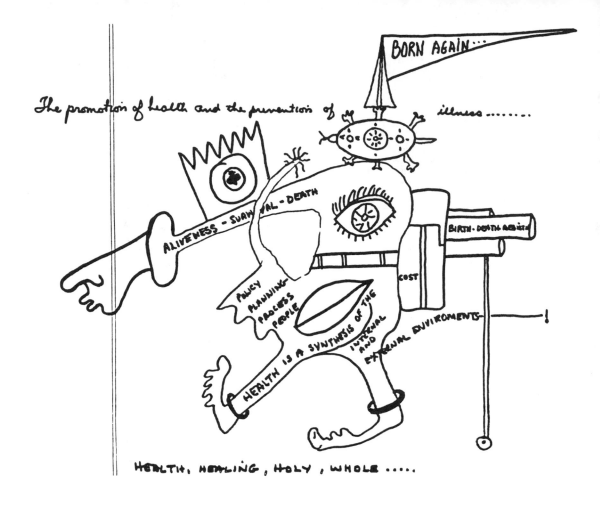

4-29 Notes from a faculty meeting.

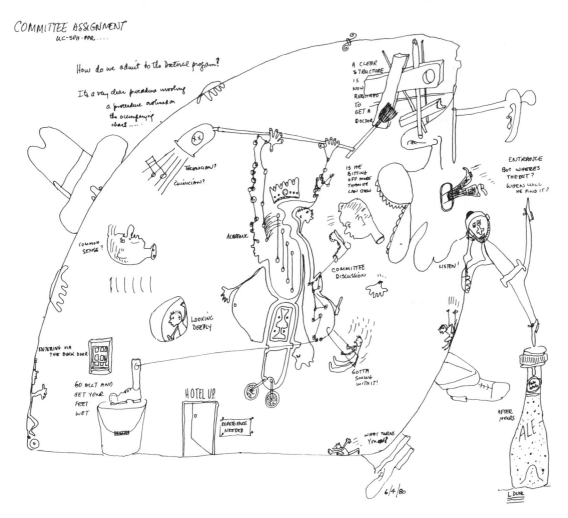

4-30 Notes for organizing a lecture.

LEONARD DUHL, M.D.
Specialist, Environmental Health

"I get bored in meetings and I doodle. For me doodling is both an art and note-taking. My thinking is nonlinear, and being dyslexic, images do better than words. Nonlinear means systems and that is what emerges as I draw: relationships, directions, emphasis. Afterwards these images remind me of what went on.

"Gradually my sketches evolved toward the use of color. And then I began using similar drawing techniques for writing. Later I used the drawings in classes both for instructing students and as a model for use in their work journals."

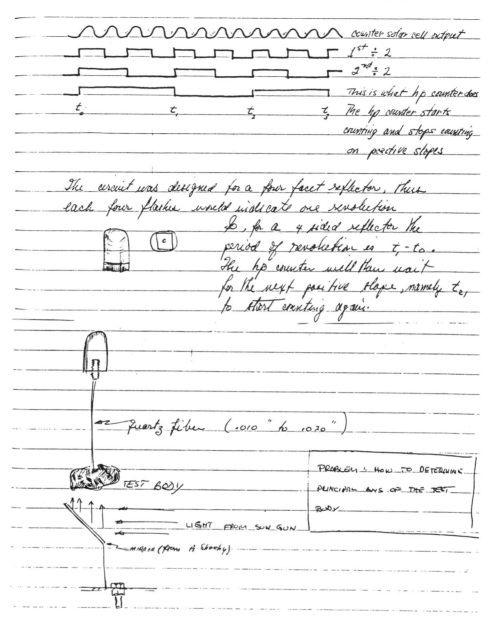

counter solar cell output

$1^{st} \div 2$

$2^{nd} \div 2$

This is what hp counter does

$t_0 \qquad t_1 \qquad t_2 \qquad t_3$ The hp counter starts counting and stops counting on positive slopes

The circuit was designed for a four facet reflector, thus each four flashes would indicate one revolution

So, for a 4 sided reflector the period of revolution is $t_1 - t_0$. The hp counter will then wait for the next positive slope, namely t_e, to start counting again.

quartz fiber (.010" to .020")

TEST BODY

LIGHT FROM SUN GUN

mirror (from A Sheehy)

PROBLEM : HOW TO DETERMINE PRINCIPAL AXIS OF THE TEST BODY

4-31 Research notes.

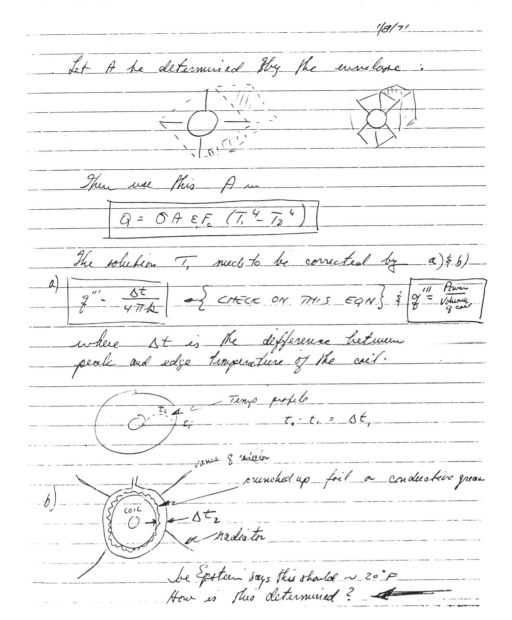

4-32 Research notes.

STEPHEN PADDACK
Aerospace Engineer/Scientist

"In research notation a few simple sketches can replace many words. The top sinusoidal wave, above, represents the responses of a solar cell used to measure rotational speed. In order to get a discreet 'edge' to measure the start of a particular spin period, a flip-flop electronic device was used which would be triggered at a certain voltage level as the current rose from zero. As you can see from the sketch, at every rising pulse the flip-flop device is triggered. The square wave has exactly one half the periodicity of the sinusoidal wave.

"The notes on the facing page are related to an electrical coil. I knew I had to have a large coil in a vacuum chamber and I was concerned about the coil getting too hot because it could not get rid of its heat. The sketches explore an idea for a device to radiate the heat away from the coil. Also I was using the classical Stephan-Boltzman radiation heat balance equation in the design."

131

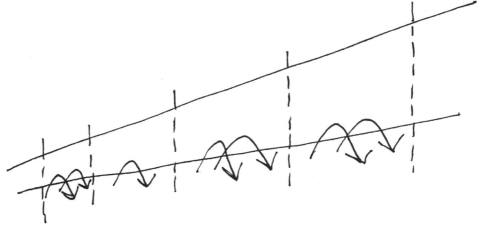

4-33A   Diachronic View of Culture.

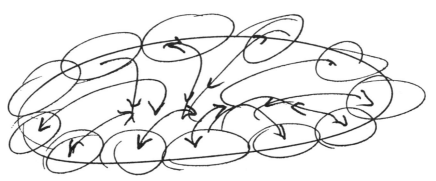

4-33B   Organic Solidarity or Functional Interdependence.

KENNETH E. MOORE
Anthropologist

"Culture can be viewed as process (diachronically) or as structure (synchronically). The first diagram illustrates culture as process. Contemporary national cultures tend to have started from smaller beginnings and to have grown over the years. The dotted lines mark off different stages, e.g., a settlement period, an expansion period, an industrializing and urbanizing period, a world power period, etc. The arrows indicate individuals who are born into a culture, whose minds are formed in the culture, in the symbolic process, who in turn contribute to the culture, then die off to be replaced by another generation. Culture in this diagram is seen as a process that can be viewed as distinct from the human beings which are its bearers. Culture is seen as a way of life based on the symbolling capacities of man. It is cumulative and it continues because man with the capacity for symbolling can transmit each generation's adaptations to succeeding generations.

"Organic Solidarity is a theoretical term of Emile Durkheim which pertains to integration in a society derived from different kinds of people, each performing destinctive functions which benefit all. Thus many specialized occupations are complementary to each other. This contrasts with the mechanical solidarity, characteristic of simple societies, in which there is only a sexual division of labor. That is, what one man knows and does, every man knows and does; what one woman knows and does, every woman knows and does."

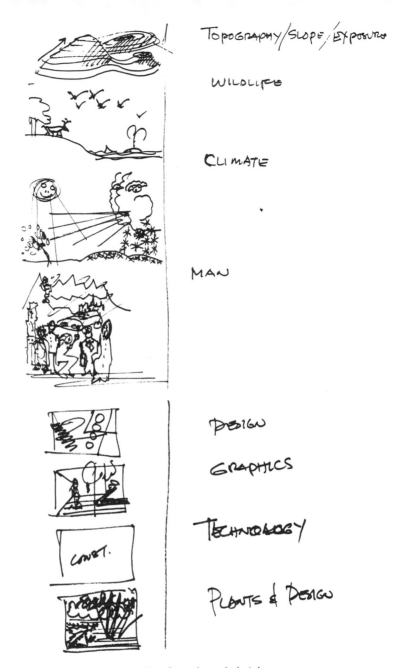

Topography/slope/exposure

Wildlife

Climate

Man

Design

Graphics

Technology

Plants & Design

4-34 Story board sketches.

JOHN RUSSELL
Landscape Architect

"These sketches were part of a story board helping me to develop the structure for a slide presentation. This technique is not unique but I would like to believe that, in the hands of a designer, the combination of graphics and narration feed on one another, providing a richer message than they would by themselves. It is very difficult for me to build this story without mental or drawn images. As I have worked more with the development of audio-visual productions, I find the relationship between drawings and words growing stronger and my story boards are beccoming more sophisticated."

DESIGN

Design notes may be the best illustrations of the range of abstraction to be found in visual notation. In design we most clearly see the impact of personal feelings and the need for an efficient and private visual language. While this first note-taker relies on an extraordinary ability to project realistic experiences, in the following examples you will see abstract notation which responds to diverse design contexts.

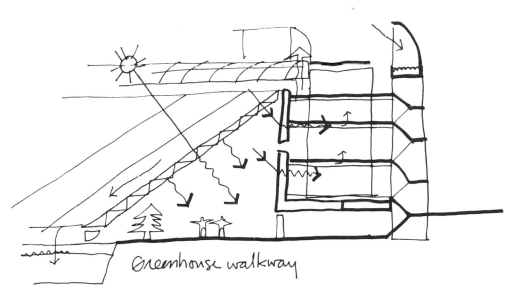

Greenhouse walkway

4-35 Sun studies for a Colorado hotel.

GENE HAYES
Architect

"I sketch to record conversations with myself and to communicate ideas to others. Sketches are much like small video cassettes, in that, when looking at a sketch, I recall what I was thinking about when I drew it and can usually go forward or backward from that point in the thought process. These sketches capture a moment in a flow of ideas that are not always directed, controlled, logical, or conscious. To me they become guideposts throughout the development of a design in that they capture the essence of an idea before it is submitted to reality and all its parameters. As design progresses the process of bringing an idea into existence becomes more complicated with more people and disciplines participating. Often one becomes so engrossed with the problems generated by the process, the basic idea or objective is forgotten, lost or mutilated beyond recognition. The sketches help me to keep my efforts centered on the original idea in order to direct and not be led by reality.

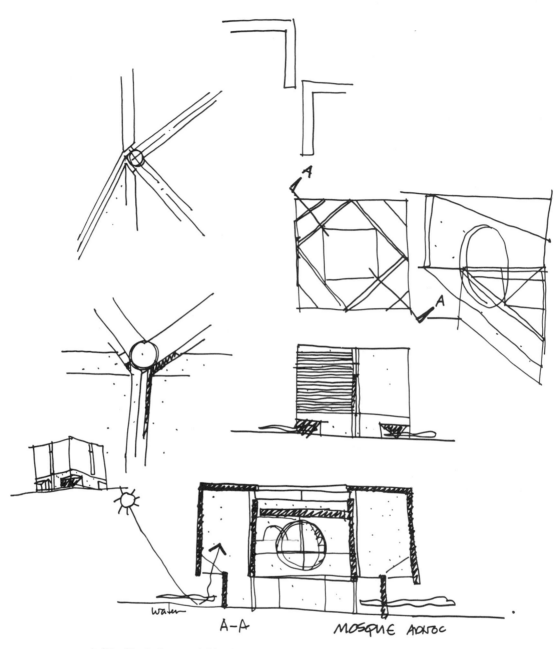

15 Jan 79

water   A-A   MOSQUE ADNOC

4-36 Study for a neighborhood mosque-Ruwais, Abu Dhabi, Saudi Arabia.

4-37 Convention center arena-Topeka, Kansas.

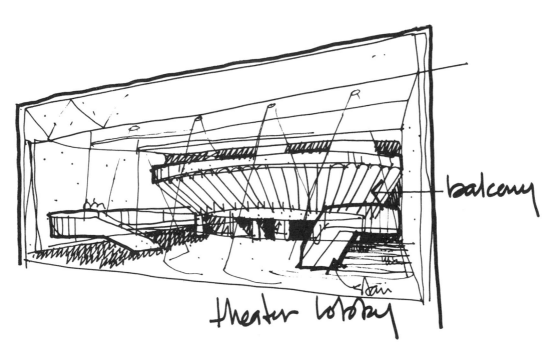

balcony

theater lobby

4-38 Convention center theatre-Topeka, Kansas.

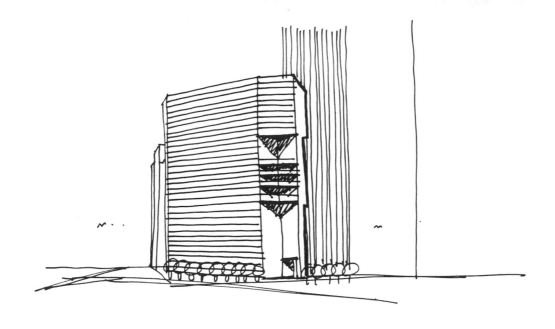

SCHEME-D *from South*   BK130 24 May 78

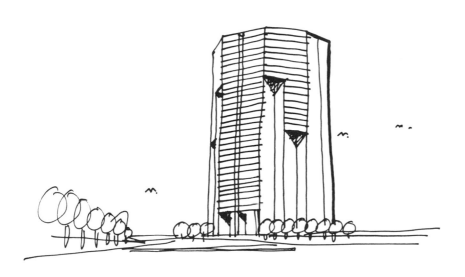

SCHEME -C *from North*   BK130 24 May 78

4-39   Massing sketches for a tower-Houston, Texas.

"I date my sketches so that I can physically reconstruct, in sequence, the design process, so I can backtrack to find a bad decision or an unexplored alternative. The creative process is by nature done in unexplored territory where it is easy to become disoriented, confused, or lost. Sketches can provide a trail to find your way and to guide others."

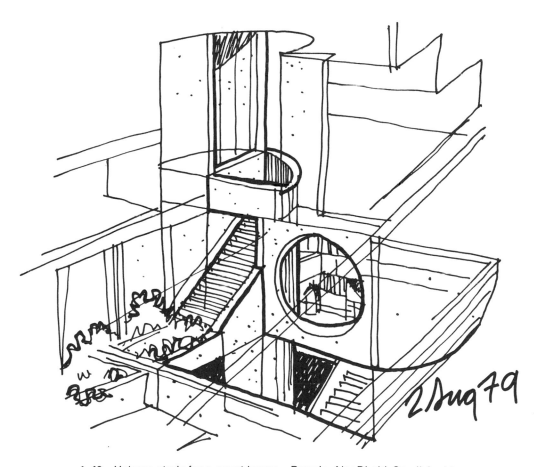

4-40 Volume study for a guest house—Ruwais, Abu Dhabi, Saudi Arabia.

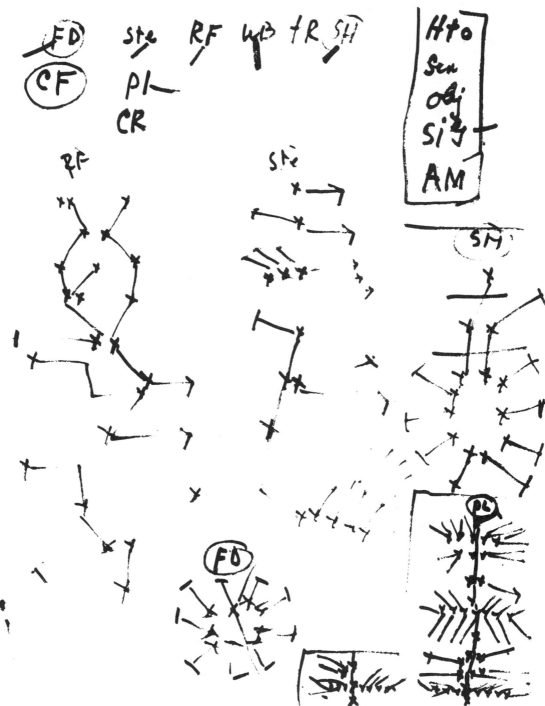

4-41 Space direction studies for dances.

MERCE CUNNINGHAM
Choreographer

"The sketches above deal with space direction possibilities for several dances, including *Rain Forrest, Field Dances, Suite for Five, Second Hand*, and *Place*. The sketches on the facing page show a space plan for camera placement to give maximum dancer visibility. The dance is *Fractions*."

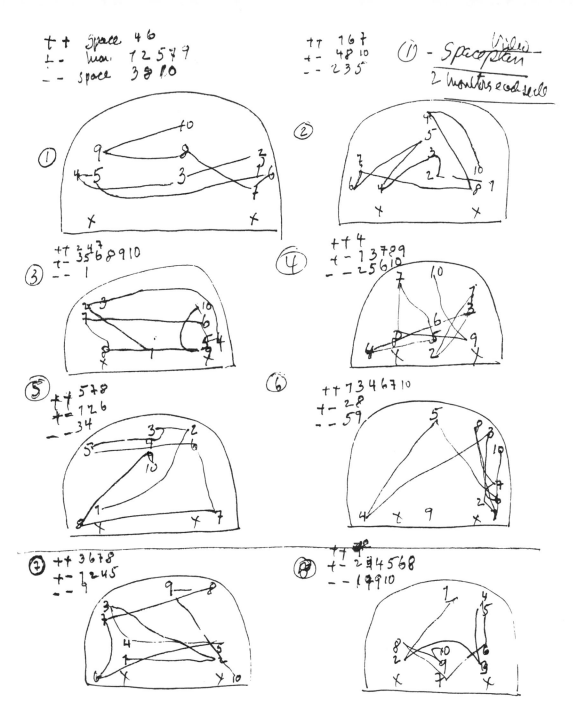

4-42 Space plan for camera placement.

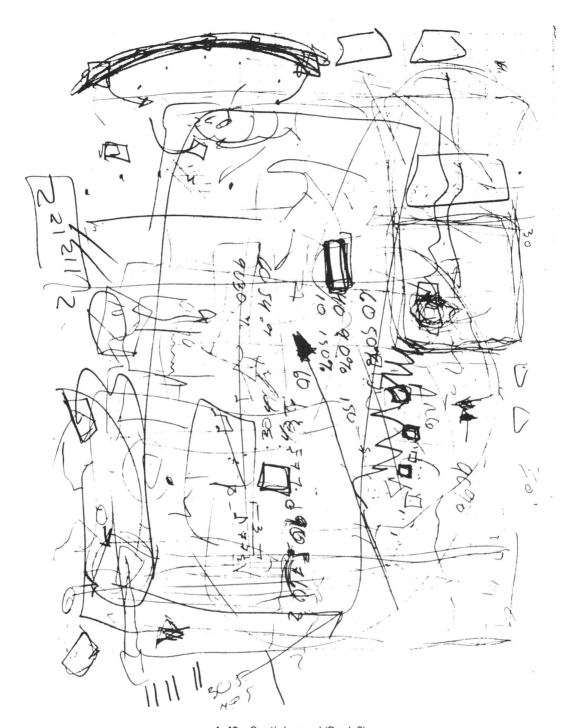

4-43 Spatial sound (Book 9).

FREDERICK BIANCHI
Music Composer

"These drawings show the beginning of my work before composition. I am just meshing ideas; one idea is put on top of another idea to the point where the idea underneath is lost. It is a conglomeration of what I have been thinking about. Within the sketch there are fragments of things which are more defined than others. The numbers are percentages; I am weighting how much I want of a certain effect or image.

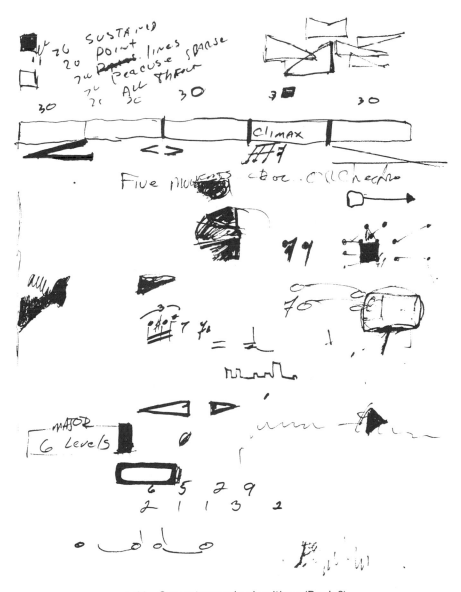

4-44 Computer music alogrithms (Book 8).

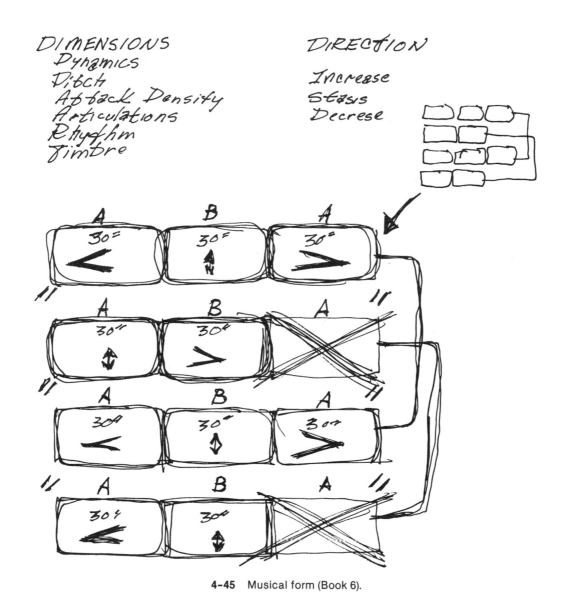

4-45 Musical form (Book 6).

"This diagram is a few steps beyond the previous sketches, but still a step before anything musical can take place such as notes or instruments. The diagram is basically organizing ideas into smaller units, indicating the direction in which I want the sound to go. Although rhythms, dynamics, pitch or other elements have not been defined, I have committed myself to a time duration and am beginning to think about the logistics of music. To me this drawing is like looking at the Rocky Mountains from far up; you see them going in certain directions and when you get down there, closer you begin to see little nooks and trees and flowers.

"The drawings on the facing page indicate the juxtaposition of ideas, events, or sounds. They show the density of the piece. They are put down so that I can begin thinking about more detailed issues such as rhythms or pitch. The sketches at the bottom of the page are not notes but just an indication of the possible density of the notes. It is a layout of how the piece will exist in time.

"I have adopted these sorts of drawings because they give me more freedom to explore and invent at the basic level of sound. They open up more possibilities."

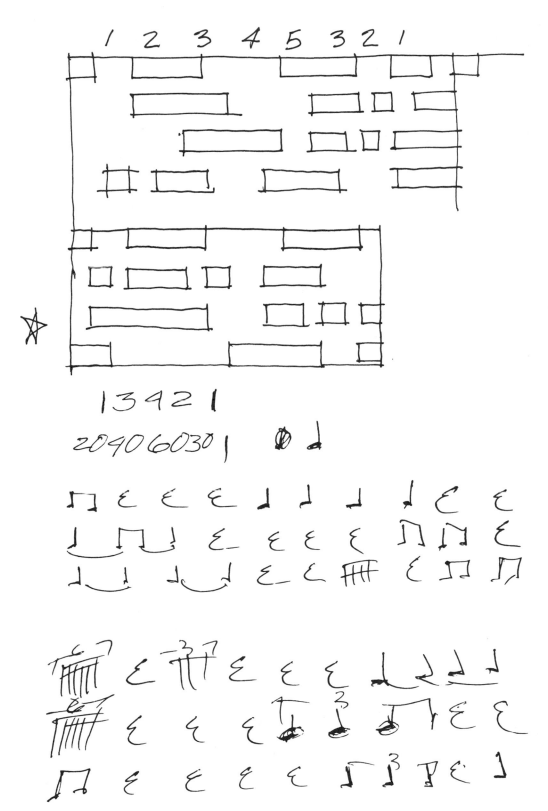

4-46 Time structures (Book 6).

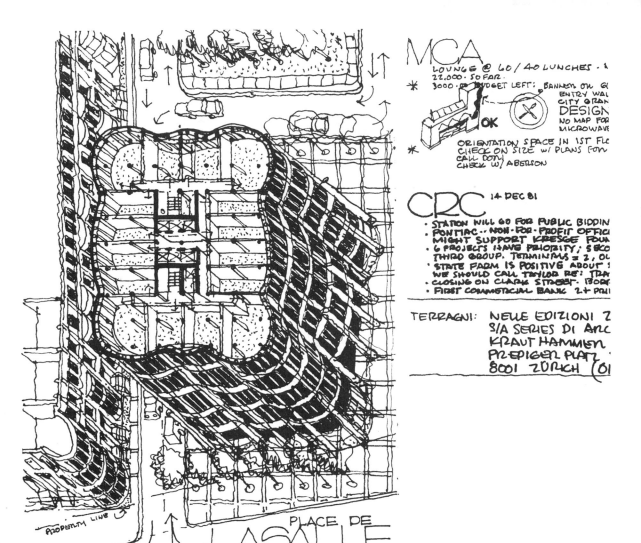

4-47 Sketch and notes for a high-rise apartment.

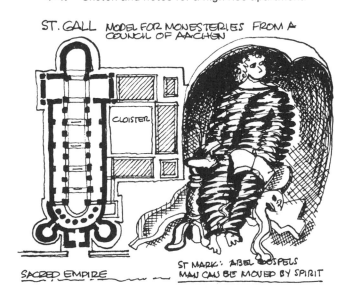

ST. GALL MODEL FOR MONESTERIES FROM A
COUNCIL OF AACHEN

CLOISTER

SACRED EMPIRE

ST MARK: ABEL GOSPELS
MAN CAN BE MOVED BY SPIRIT

4-48 Notes on Medieval art.

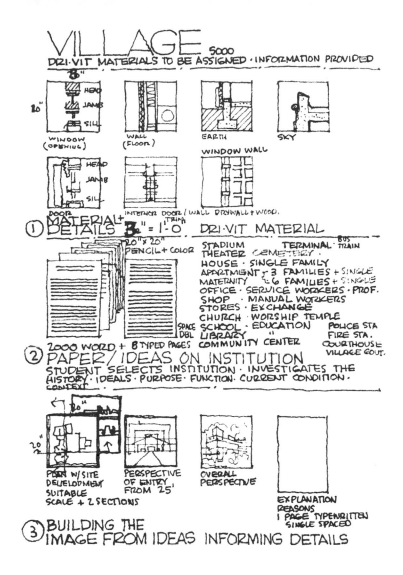

4-49 Notes for a class at the University of Illinois.

LAURENCE BOOTH
Architect

The example here with which we close this chapter may, at first sight, seem too accomplished to provide a practical or realistic model for the average person. But if you look closely and calmly at these sketches, we believe that you will see that their quality derives primarily from the care and patience of a designer who truly enjoys his work and from his desire to be as clear and direct as possible in communicating his ideas. His drawings are intense, not magic.

Tools and Techniques

5-1

This chapter pulls together a number of practical suggestions for equipment and note-taking which we have gathered from our own experience and the experience of accomplished designers in the course of writing this book. These notes are intended as an easy reference for the beginner or someone who is brushing up on skills first acquired some time ago.

These techniques are covered in more detail in a number of books. We have provided an annotated bibliography at the conclusion of the book to help you find those techniques of most interest to you.

Equipment

    The Notebook
    Pens, Pencils, and Other Equipment

Basic Drawings

    Notebook Entries
    Field Sketches
    Gridded Paper

    Line Drawings
    Values/Tones
    Detail/Pattern
    People

Conventions

    Elevations
    Plans/Sections
    Paraline Drawings
    Perspectives
    Transparencies
    Disassemblies

Analytical Drawings

    Geometry
    Zoning
    Contrasts
    Rhythms
    Proportions

Symbolic Drawings

    Symbols
    Diagrams
    Area Diagram/Matrix/Network

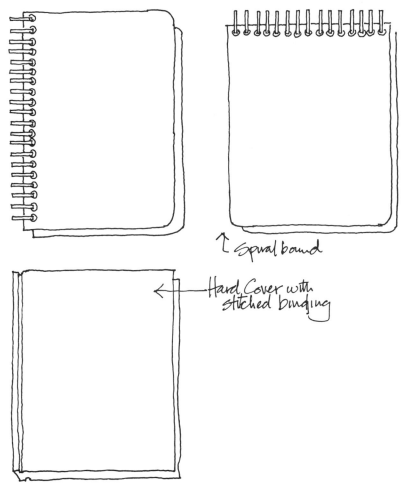

Spiral bound

Hard Cover with
Stitched binding

5-2 Basic notebooks.

The Notebook

Many designers who keep visual notes have given some thought to their choice of notebook. Although different designers will have special requirements or preferences, there are some general considerations in selecting a notebook:

1. Durability: notebooks should be a permanent record and therefore able to endure the effects of continuous use and storage for at least a lifetime. They should contain good quality paper protected by a heavy cover which is not easily bent or torn.

2. Portability: you will want to have your notebook accessible at all times, so select one which can be easily carried with you. A pocket-sized book is the most portable, but if you are in the habit of keeping a brief-case or sketchbook bag with you, a larger notebook may also be convenient.

3. Utility: if a notebook is difficult to use you probably will not use it, thus defeating its purpose. Notebooks which are too thick or too large are hard to hold or carry. A spiral binding can be helpful because the rigid cover and used pages can be turned completely back making the notebook much easier to hold.

4. Visibility: to be most effective, drawings and notes should be easy to see. Generally pencil shows well on paper with a tooth to

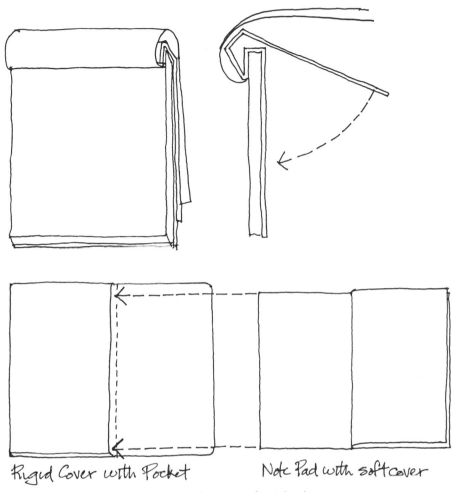

Rigid Cover with Pocket   Note Pad with soft cover

5-3 Alternative types of notebooks.

it, while ink works best on smoothly finished papers. Paper which is too porous will spread ink or snag the point of the pen resulting in fuzzy, irregular lines. Paper that is too thin may tear or let ink bleed through to the next page.

There are a variety of notebooks available; we have found two basic types to be the most effective. The first is bound with a wire spiral at the top or the side, is about 3 $\frac{1}{2}$ inches wide, 5–6 inches high, and less than $\frac{1}{2}$ inch thick, with a stiff cardboard front and back cover. The second type of notebook is stitch-bound with a stiff cover and about the same size but not quite as thick. Other options include: a removable protective cover into which soft cover

notebooks can be inserted, and a rigid back cover with a soft front cover which can be folded over the top of the pad.

Notebooks are manufactured with a variety of papers. We recommend a highly opaque paper with a smooth finish; this should allow crisp drawings which do not show through to the other side of the page. Some designers prefer transparent papers so that they can retrace sketches. Others use paper with light blue grids to assist drawing. You should experiment and find the notebook that most suits your way of working. If what you want is not available, it is not difficult to have notebooks made to your order.

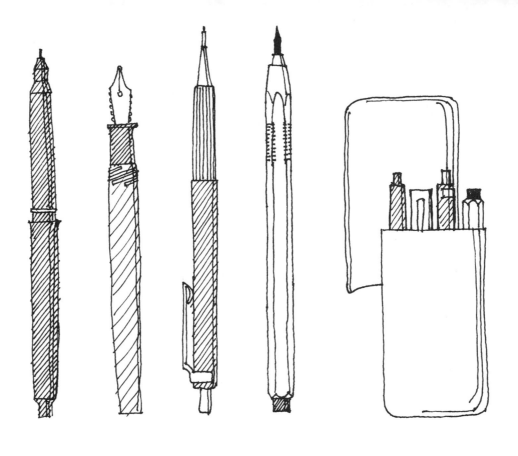

5-4 Basic drawing instruments.

Pens, Pencils and Other Equipment

Ink is the preferable media for notebooks because of its permanence and high visibility; it also encourages the note-taker to develop skill at rapid, accurate drawing. There are many brands of fine-line markers which produce a clear, dark line and are convenient to carry. The cartridge ink pen is a good option for people who prefer a more fluid line; it has the added advantage of being less susceptible to blotching or bleeding through the paper.

Used skillfully, the pencil can also be effective in visual note-taking. It has the advantage of being able to produce a wide range of values from light to dark but is not as permanent as ink and may smudge. If you use a pencil, do not use hard leads or rely on erasers; as a rule it is better to start the drawing over instead of attempting to correct the original drawing. Some designers carry a few colored pencils to provide more options in their drawings; however, broad-tip markers are not very practical for notebooks because they bleed through the paper and spread so that they are difficult to control.

Most of us have had holes punched in pockets or stains caused by pens or pencils. Some people carry sketching equipment in a camera bag or attache case. A less cumbersome option is a leather cigar holder which can easily be carried in a jacket pocket and protects the pens and pencils as well as your clothing.

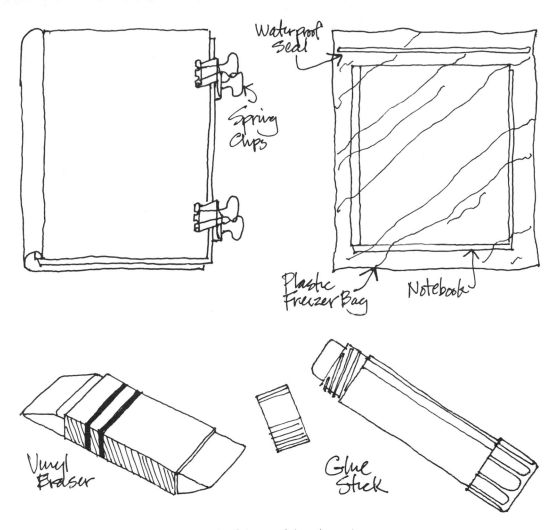

Waterproof Seal

Spring Clips

Plastic Freezer Bag

Notebook

Vinyl Eraser

Glue Stick

5-5 Other useful equipment.

Other handy equipment includes: a soft vinyl eraser; binder clips to hold back notebook pages; a thin plastic 6 inch ruler and a sealable plastic freezer bag to protect your notebook from rain or moisture.

Occasionally in your travels you may come across a little map or other printed material which is very effective in describing an idea, and taking the time to recopy it in your notebook does not make sense. Or you may have a little sketch on a napkin or tracing paper which you wish to save. You can quickly secure such papers in you notebook with a portable paste stick. Rub the back of the paper and press into the book.

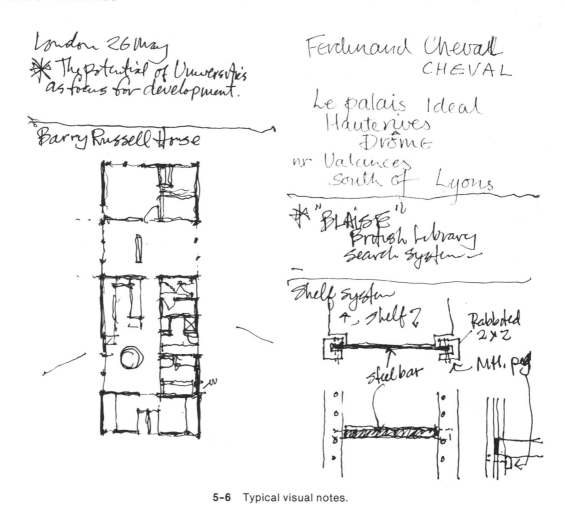

5-6   Typical visual notes.

Notebook Entries

When they first start a notebook, some people feel that each new idea or subject has to go on a new page. They find that they are quickly filling their notebooks, leaving many half-used pages. A simple way to avoid this is drawing a line across the page at the end of each thought or idea before starting a new idea. Although this often results in several different ideas clustered on one page, you will be able to distinguish them from each other, and thinking is stimulated by observing relationsips between different ideas within the same page.

Lines can also be useful for separating ideas in larger notebooks by creating smaller areas and thereby forcing yourself to be more compact and economical with sketches. Dating entries to a sketchbook helps keep track of the origin or context of an idea. Long after you have forgotten the names of related people or places, you will probably remember the approximate date on which you heard a speaker or visited a place. By going back through the sketchbooks chronologically you can quickly relocate the idea.

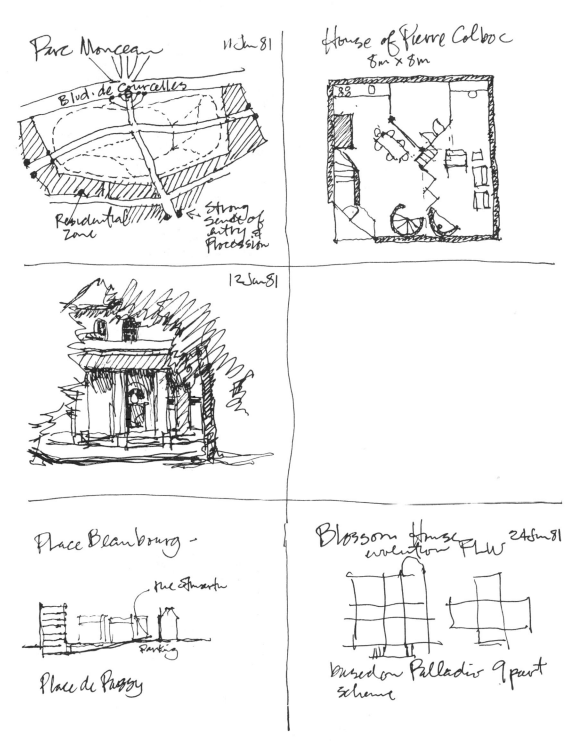

5-7 Organizing the notes.

Tree Canopy

Grass

Pink & Red Yellow Flowers

Shaded Lanes

5-8 Original field sketch.

5-9 Sketch enlargement.

5-10 Rough pencil sketch drawn over in pen.

Field Sketches

One difficulty which most note-takers face is a lack of time to draw a subject. To deal with this, rapidly sketch in the general forms and make notes about other features such as values, patterns, or details (see Line Drawing in this chapter), then recreate the drawing at a later time by referring to your notes. You may also make a rough drawing in pencil and later draw over it in pen, then remove the pencil with a soft eraser. Keep your notebook nearby at all times. Get into the habit of noting your ideas no matter where or when you get them. Some people get most of their ideas in special settings or times such as just before they go to sleep or when they wake up. Write the date on the cover of each notebook when you start it and when you complete it. Keep all your notebooks together in one safe place.

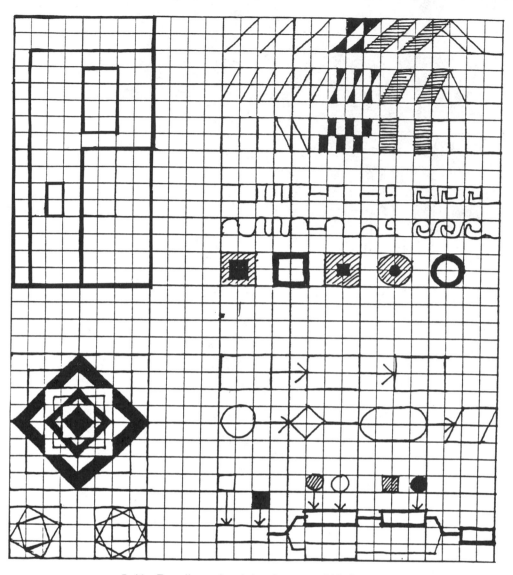

5-11 Two dimensional drawings on gridded paper.

Gridded Paper

Some people use notebooks with gridded paper. Pads with $\frac{1}{10}''$, $\frac{1}{8}''$, or $\frac{1}{4}''$ light blue grids are available. The grid can be useful in a number of ways in making sketches. It assists in accurately portraying proportions or redundant rhythms in a quick sketch. The grid facilitates drawing certain angles, such as a 45 or 90 degree. One can quickly increase or reduce the scale of a drawing. The grid is convenient for constructing diagrams and conventional drawings such as paraline projections.

5-12 Enlargements and three-dimensional drawings.

5-13 Grain silos—Indiana.

Line Drawings

Learning how to draw representationally is the most effective and rewarding way to learn how to observe and take notes. The objective is not to become an "artist" but to learn how to make representative drawings which are well within the potential of us all. Anyone can learn to draw, if they understand the mental blocks to drawing and learn to overcome those blocks while developing the skills of observation. Drawings are usually time-consuming for the beginner, so be sure to start with subjects which are interesting. Take some time to look around for available subjects. They should have some complexity so that you do not get bored half-way through the drawing; try a historical area in the city, an industrial complex, a shipyard, or grain silos, depending on the part of the country in which you live.

5-14 Charleston, South Carolina.

5-15 Harbor crane—Milwaukee.

5-16 The Basilica and Piazza dei Signori—Vicenza, Italy.

5-17

5-18

5-19 A preliminary sketch of the Basilica with ordering lines exaggerated.

Walk around the site; observe how the relationship or composition of shapes and the patterns of shadows change as you move. Pick a view of a subject which is interesting. Look at the subject for awhile; try to see how it is composed. Are there dominating horizontal or vertical forms? Are they to one side or in the center of the view? Are there any other dominant features? Are there large dark or light areas such as sky, sea, ground, or wall? What is their shape? Now begin drawing by first indicating the correct position of the large elements. These can then be used as a "map" for positioning the smaller parts of the subject. If, at first, you find the subject too complicated or too large to keep track of all relationships, your first drawing might include a smaller portion of the subject. This initial line drawing is the basic structure upon which all the other information must hang, so take your time and try to get each part at the right size and in its proper place.

5-20 Final sketch of the Basilica.

5-21 Partial elevation.

5-22

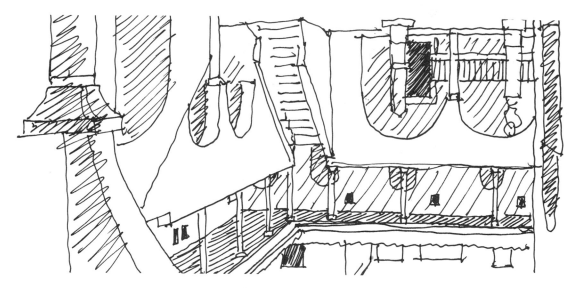

5-23 Courtyard—Hydra, Greece.

These initial line drawings can be the source of frustration for the beginners because they have self-doubts or are overly critical of their first attempts and because the symbolic, verbal part of their brain is fighting to maintain dominance. If this is a problem there are a few specific things that can be done to help.

Reversals: Find a slide or a photo of an interesting subject and view it upside down. This will help defeat the brain's attempt to symbolize or rationalize and allow the brain to apply its observational capabilities. Allow plenty of time for these first drawings, avoid distractions and do not put pressures on yourself. Relax and enjoy the view. Most people are pleasantly surprised by the realistic quality of these "upside-down drawings" and find the step to normal-view drawings to be easier.

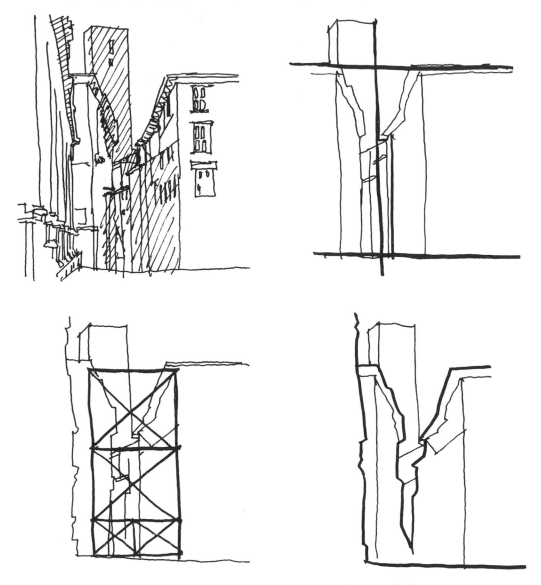

5-24   Organizing sketches, Citta Alta, Bergamo, Italy.

References: Another aid is the use of organizing lines or grids. Look for one vertical and one horizontal edge or form somewhere near the center of the view; draw vertical and horizontal lines at these places which extend across the view. This will divide the view into quadrants, making it easier to position the different parts of the subject. Using a similar approach, look for parts of the view which form an imaginary square; lightly sketch in the square and, as before, use the square as a reference for locating the parts of the subject. You can also pick out three or four prominent points in the view, carefully draw them in their proper relationship, and use them as reference points.

General Shapes: Another useful method for developing line drawings begins with identifying large zones of the view. These zones may be large objects, groups of objects, or the voids between objects. If they are large enough in relation to the whole drawing, you need to identify only one or two of these zones. Carefully draw the contour of the zone(s); if the contour is not accurate or the proportions of the zone are bad, you can afford to start over again on a new sheet of paper. Once these shapes are properly drawn, it is a simpler task to complete the rest of the line drawing.

5-25   Citta Alta, Bergamo, Italy.

Values/Tones

Having completed the line drawing of the parts of the subject the representational qualities of the drawing can be enhanced through the indication of values by applying tones to the drawing. Values are the lightness or darkness of surfaces as they are seen; this may be due to the color or the degree of light or shadow which falls upon them. Tones often help in identifying objects but they are also very helpful in representing three-dimensional space. Tones can be applied by a number of media, but, as with most of the descriptions in this book we will emphasize the use of

line-based techniques in order to keep the necessary tools to a minimum. The simplest technique for creating tones is the use of evenly spaced parallel lines. The value (degree or darkness) of the tone is controlled by the spacing of the lines (the closer the lines are to each other the darker the tone). The other consideration in applying tones is the direction of the parallel lines. As a general rule, avoid vertical tone lines as they can be confused with vertical lines in the basic drawing; for vertical surfaces use diagonal lines and for horizontal surfaces use horizontal lines.

5-26

5-27

5-28

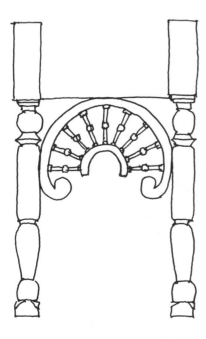

Detail/Pattern

The third concern of a representational drawing is the specific shapes of parts of the subject. These may be singular items such as a street lamp or lettering on a sign, or they may be typical shapes in a pattern such as the tiles on a roof, the posts in a railing or fence, or the brick pattern in a wall. Most of us are overwhelmed when faced with indicating repetitive forms in a roof or a tree; confronted with this tedious task we try to rush through it, scribbling symbolic forms. There is an easy way out of this mess: make a careful note of one or two of the shapes in each pattern and then fill in the rest of the pattern at a later time when you will have no need to rush.

5-29 Cappella Colleoni—Citta Alta, Bergamo, Italy.

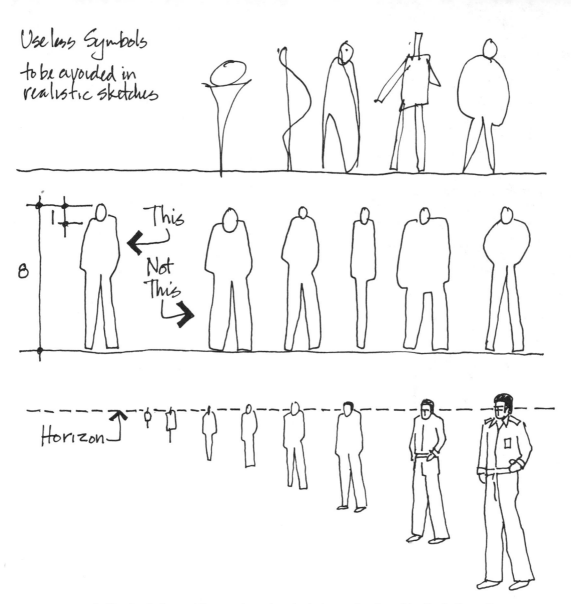

Useless Symbols
to be avoided in
realistic sketches

This

Not This

8

Horizon

5-30 Basic human figures, based on techniques developed by Kevin Forseth.

People

Many of us shy away from indicating people in environments unless it is absolutely necessary to establish scale or some notion of activity. And yet people are a very important part of describing experiences and understanding our relationships to environments. For this reason, it is useful to establish some minimal techniques for indicating relatively realistic people within our drawings. The first condition for realistic figures is that of scale. Figures must be in scale with their environment, and figures themselves must be proportioned so that the scale of any part, especially the head, is proper to that of the body. The second consideration is that of simplicity. The more distant the figure or

person is from the observer, the less detail we are able to see; in many cases, we can only discern shape and overall proportion. The third consideration is animation. At any given time, people are often in the process of moving in an environment. Even when they are at rest, there is a kind of dynamic balance suggested. To understand this, observe and sketch people in real life; look at how cartoonists achieve this sense of dynamics, or animation. The last consideration is that of placement of people within an environment, where they congregate, or how they move through it, so you need to do some looking in order to realistically depict people in environments.

5-31 Human figures within environments.

5-32 Evolution of an elevation sketch.

Elevations

Usually as frontal views of building walls, elevations are rapid ways to record both the order and the character of a building or an exterior space. This drawing convention shows all of the elements of the facade of the building as if they had all been pressed onto a single flat plane. There is little sense of perspective or depth. The first step in making such a drawing is to carefully observe the dimensions of the facade, so that you can accurately represent the overall proportions of the building. Next, look for major subdivisions in the facade that create subzones, and finally place windows and other openings or features within those subzones. This process of going from the general to the particular allows you to keep the drawing well-proportioned and accurate.

The elevation in combination with a section drawing is a particularly useful convention. You get the benefit of understanding the order and character of spatial enclosure while obtaining some sense of the definition of three-dimensional space. Other types of elevation show all faces of a building in one drawing, revealing a comprehensive view, or show elevations of several walls which are experienced in a progression, providing an understanding of the relationships among parts of a building.

5-33 Final sketch of Chenonceaux—Loire Valley, France.

5-34 Cloister—Certosa di Pavia, Italy.

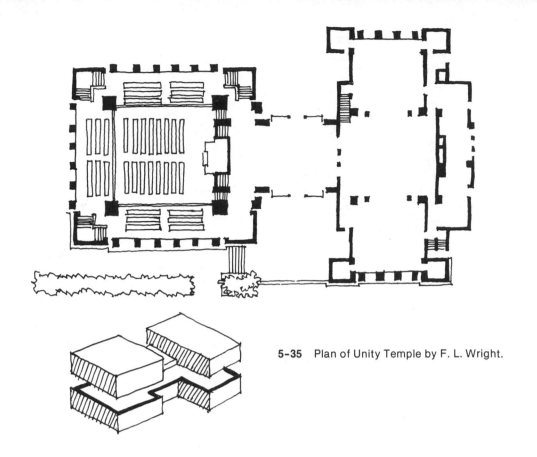

5-35   Plan of Unity Temple by F. L. Wright.

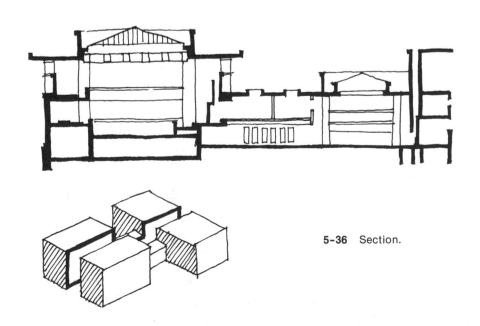

5-36   Section.

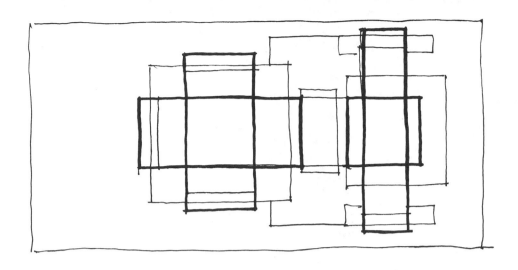

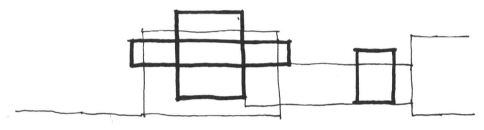

5-37   Abstract plan and section.

Plan/Section

The conventional "plan" drawing represents the view of a building when a cut is made through the building and the top removed, revealing the bottom half. Strictly speaking, this is a plan section. The conventional "section" drawing shows an elevation view resulting from a vertical cut through a building; it is more accurately described as an elevation section. In both the elevation section and plan section it is important to distinguish those things which have been cut through from those things which are beyond the section. This is usually indicated by heavy outlining of the parts which have been cut. Plan sections are useful in gaining an understanding of buildings or objects. But their utility extends beyond realistic representation. Plan diagrams in which walls are represented as single lines or in which general territories or zones are identified are quick ways of describing the conceptual order of a given environment or designed object. They are also helpful in describing scale and relationships between parts.

175

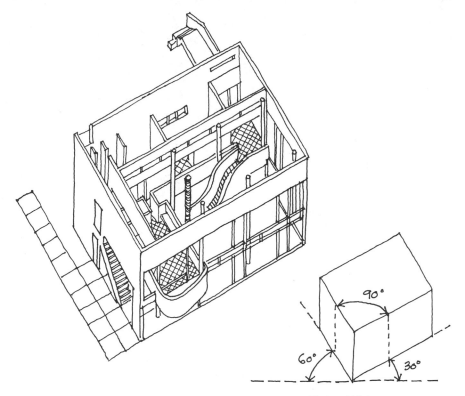

5-38 Plan oblique, Shamberg House by Richard Meier.

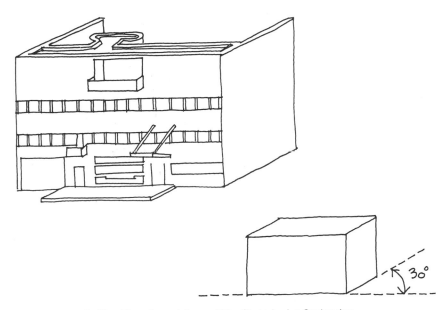

5-39 Elevation oblique, Villa Stein by Le Corbusier.

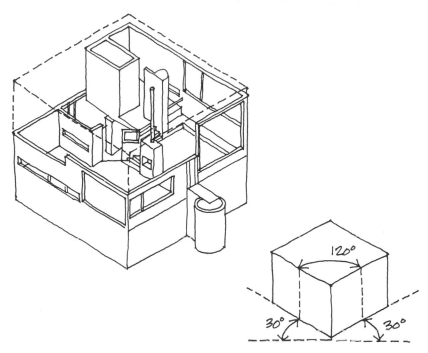

5-40 Isometric, Simon House by Barbara and Julian Neski.

Paraline Drawings

These are drawings which are the basic alternate convention to perspective projection for representing three-dimensional space or objects. In paraline projections, all lines which are parallel in space are shown parallel in the drawing. There are three basic types of paraline projections: the plan oblique (commonly referred to as an axonometric); the elevation oblique; and the isometric.

A plan oblique projection is essentially a plan view from which walls or other elements are extended vertically to create the sensation of three-dimensional space and to illustrate information about the vertical surfaces. This convention places the plan on an angle, generally somewhere around 30 or 60 degrees from the horizontal. Vertical lines are then drawn from various points on the plan to describe the walls. All the measurements of pieces in the plan oblique are at the same scale making them easier to construct than perspectives which we will discuss later.

The elevation oblique is constructed in the same manner as the plan oblique except that an elevation of a wall or vertical sur-

face is drawn first and then the horizontal surfaces and other vertical surfaces are projected at an angle from the elevation. People who are used to drawing perspectives of buildings will often have difficulty in sketching oblique projections particularly in keeping the angled lines parallel. One way to overcome this is to draw the true plan or elevation views first, concentrating on keeping lines perpendicular to each other and then sketch in the parallel projection lines. Gridded paper is handy for this purpose. By simply using a convention of one space over for every two up, it is possible to quickly draw parallel lines and achieve minimal distortion of scale for both plan and elevation lines.

Isometric projections essentially illustrate all surfaces in the three dimensions with equal distortion. The construction grid for isometrics consists of the vertical line, a line 60 degrees to the right of the vertical and a line of 60 degrees to the left of the vertical. Of the paraline drawings the isometric most closely approaches the realistic impression of perspective drawings.

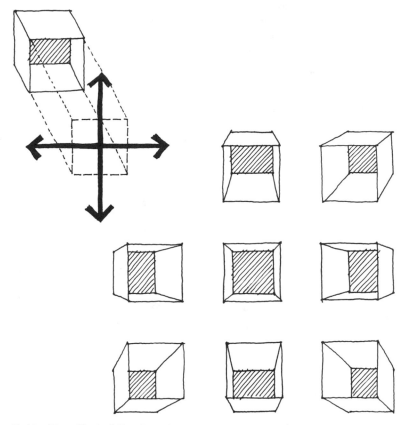

5-41　The effect of the viewer's movement on one-point perspective views.

Perspectives

There is a sense of the depth and relationships experienced in three-dimensional environments, which perspective as a convention attempts to simulate. Generally speaking, as you attempt to draw three-dimensional spaces from real life, you will begin to acquire this "sense" of perspective, upon which you can commonly rely to represent three-dimensional space; you must draw in order to learn to draw. However, in the course of your experiences both in gathering information and in creating designs for new environments you are often called upon to draw three-dimensional spaces which do not yet exist or which you cannot see. For this purpose, some simple rules for constructing one-point perspectives can be handy. The convention of one-point perspective is based on the rules that apply when one is observing an environment or an object from a single point in space. For this reason, it is first important to understand the effect of the location of the observer on the view and the perspective drawing. First let us see how the location of the observer is the principal determining factor in constructing a perspective. Using a cube as our object we can see how different observation points above and below or at the same level as the cube or moving from left to right affect the drawing of the perspective. If we then change the scale of the cube relative to ourselves, the cube can become an environment; and we can see the effect on the view of our being in different positions looking at that environment. As a general rule, perspective views, whether of objects or of spaces should be based upon observation points from which you would normally see them. So an ashtray is normally viewed from above as it sits on a table whereas a living room would be experienced from a standing or seated position.

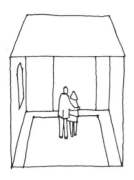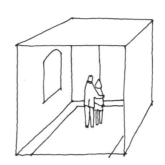

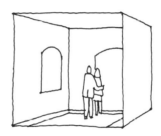

5-42

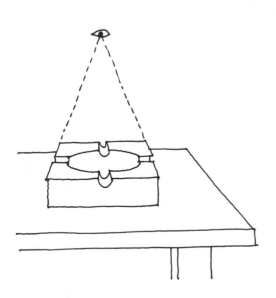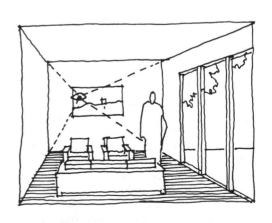

5-43 Construction of simple one-point perspective sketches based on the location of the viewer.

a. Vertical position.
b. Position left to right.
c. Distance from the subject.

In constructing a perspective, the first important step is to establish the position of the observer by indications in the drawing itself. The first component of position is the vertical relationship, namely, the elevation in space of the observer's eye relative to the object or the space being viewed. This is indicated by the "horizon line." The next component to be indicated is the horizontal or left to right relationship indicated on the horizon by a "station point." Finally you want to indicate the distance between the observer and the object or space. Although this position cannot be indicated on the drawing itself, it will have an effect on the perspective. To account for this distance, we will indicate a point on the horizon line to either left or right of the station point which at the scale of the drawing will be equal to the distance we are away from that object. We can understand the effect of using this point by illustrating two different situations in which the observer is at different distances from a space and seeing how the diagonal generated from that point creates different views of the bottom of the space.

Once you understand the convention of perspective, you will be concerned with indicating the proportion, scale, and location of objects within a space. To deal with this, we draw a three-dimensional grid. For sketching, it is not necessary to have a very elaborate grid; in fact, the simpler, the better. If we know the size of the major grid that we have made, it is a simple matter to position various elements within this grid. In a sketch, it is unnecessary to establish extremely accurate dimensions. Construction of this three-dimensional grid is fairly easy, using the horizon lines, vanishing point, and station point explained earlier. The basic steps for construction of the grid are illustrated to the right.

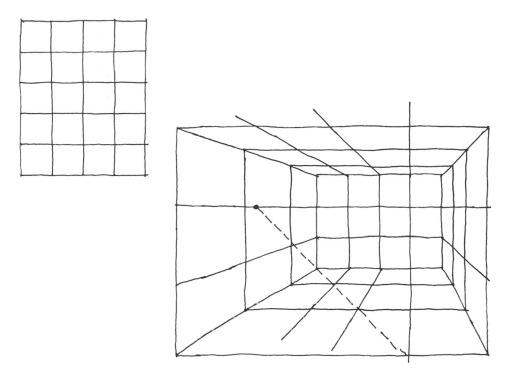

5-44 Basic grid for plan and perspective.

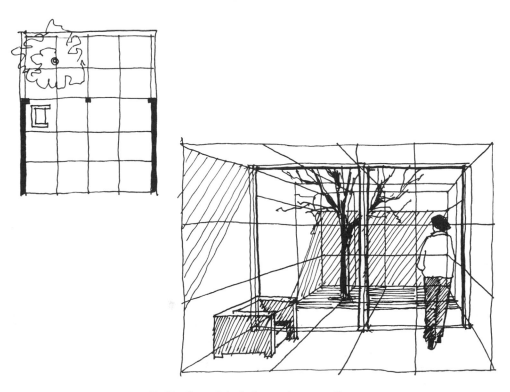

5-45 Completed plan and perspective.

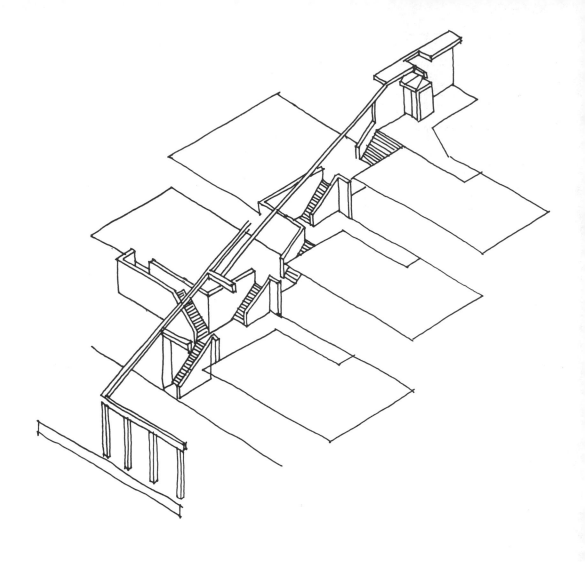

5-46 Bookstaver House by Peter Glick.

Transparencies

Sometimes it is important to show the relationship between the exterior and the interior of an object or building. One of the ways to do this is to treat all or some of the walls as if they were transparent by either removing them totally or by showing the dotted outline of the walls that have been removed. It is often helpful to darken-in the portion of walls that have been cut away to show where the wall would have been. The effect of the transparency can be heightened by contrasting the interior with the exterior portions of the building through the use of tones or contour lines. Because of the complex nature of this sort of view, it is best to keep these illustrations simple with minimal rendering to give maximum legibility; avoid the use of squiggly or irregular cut lines through planes.

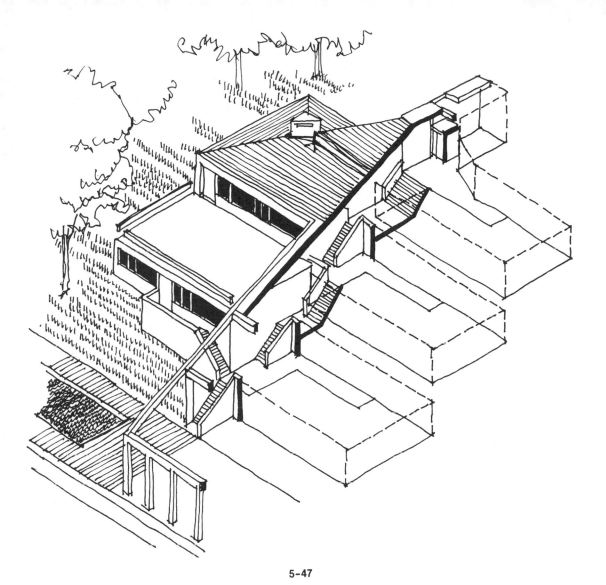

5-47

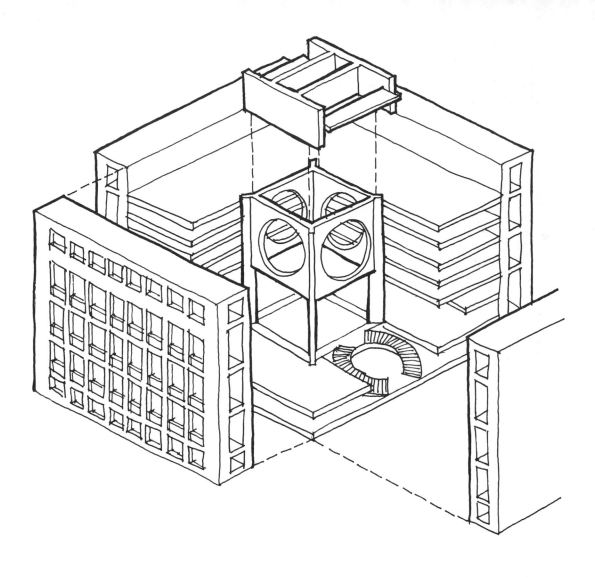

5-48 Exeter Academy Library by Louis I. Kahn.

Disassemblies

These show an object or building
disassembled with the parts in such a position that you can see how they can be
reassembled. The use of axes or dotted
lines can indicate the path along which the
pieces move as they fit together. This helps
people understand the parts more clearly
and appreciate the forming of the whole.
This type of drawing is sometimes referred
to as an explodametric because it appears
to have been blown apart.

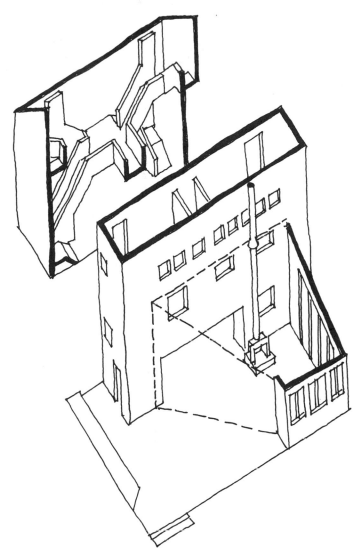

5-49 Tatum House by MTLW/Turnbull Associates.

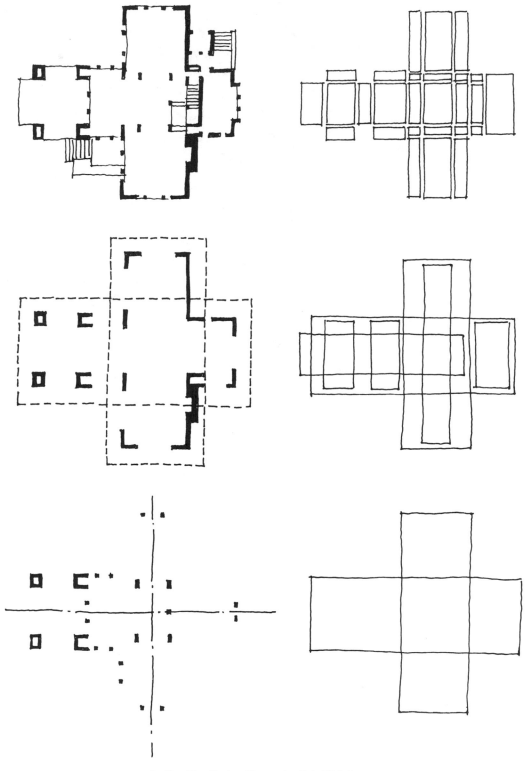

5-50 The Barton House by F. L. Wright.

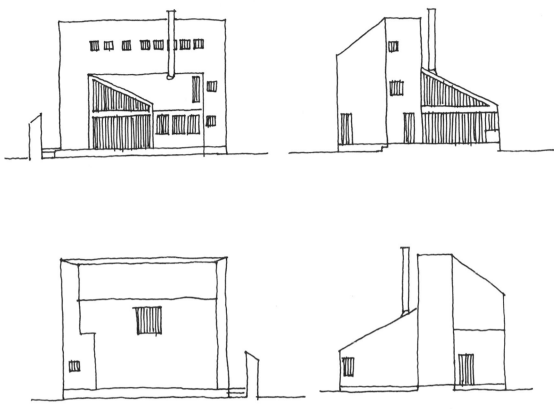

5-51 Fenestration studies of Tatum House by MTLW/Turnbull Associates.

The following techniques are ones used specifically for drawings which attempt to be analytical rather than representational. There is not a right or wrong way to do these drawings, but the following examples can give you some idea of at least one way of going about it. These are different than representational or realistic drawings because they are intentionally abstract, attempting to distill ideas or experiences and to focus on specific elements of that reality.

Geometry

As designers we are often concerned with understanding the underlying structure of a given form or object. One way of expressing this order is to abstract or identify an inherent geometry such as a building having either a radial, axial, or linear plan. Analytical drawings which show geometry can be useful at a variety of scales from the building up to city or regional planning and from building scale down to a window or floor pattern. In doing this type of analytical drawing, one would first look for an organizing grid or set of lines in a plan or facade, for example, then illustrate the subdivisions within those basic grids. In addition one would be looking for correspondences between the heights or relative scales of different parts.

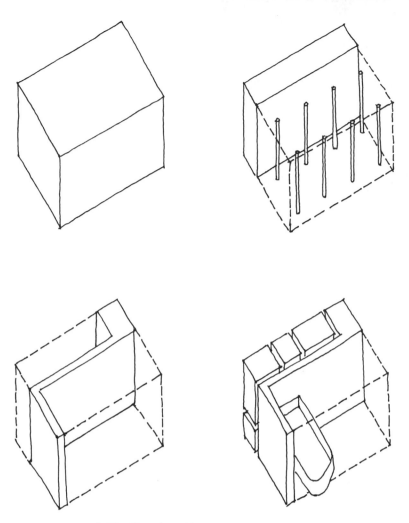

5-52 Shamberg House by Richard Meier.

Zoning

Probably the most basic distinguishing factor in a building is the manner in which major program functions are distributed in spaces. In noting the zoning pattern for a given building we come to understand basic ways in which functions can relate to each other and in which they can be organized and reconciled on a large scale. Most often these kinds of zoning diagrams are represented in a plan view. However, it is possible to show vertical zoning either represented as a sort of section or elevation. A three-dimensional zoning diagram in which you create volumes of space devoted to functions is perhaps most useful.

5-53 Maison Shodan by Le Corbusier.

Contrasts

The major way of distinguishing elements of the environment around us is to see their relative lightness and darkness or color *value.* This is the way in which certain things stand out from their background, such as the branches of a tree against the sky. Often a sketch of a scene done completely in tones without lines can do an excellent job of conveying the spatial quality of that building, extracting it out of the context of the details and other features of the building. The contrast of light and dark in turn can clarify the pattern of elements in the building, such as rows of windows in a facade. A rule of thumb in working with this kind of drawing is to first identify darkest elements, and then the very lightest elements, then ask yourself how many variations of value there are between those extremes. Generally speaking, an analytical drawing should depict no more than five different value levels. The lightest and darkest tones are put into the drawing first and then the other tones added.

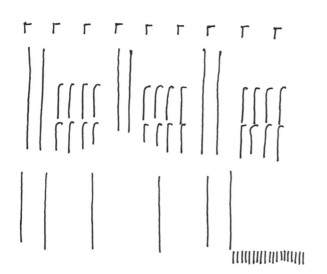

5-54 Cambridge, England.

Rhythms

Another type of drawing indicates the relationships between parts as they form certain rhythms in the facade. You will find that there are some larger scale repetitions or redundancies in a building, and that there are also some smaller scale pieces that create additional rhythms. If the analytical drawing is shown next to the representational drawing of the same view, we can see the elements of the building which are creating these rhythms. Generally speaking, this type of abstract drawing should be of a high contrast so that the rhythms can be more clearly seen.

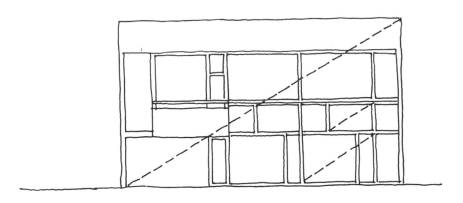

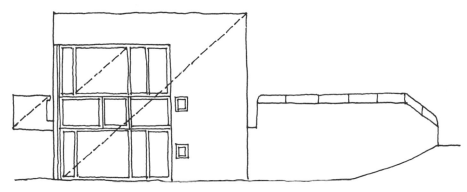

5-55 Shamberg House by Richard Meier.

Proportions

A sense of unity in a building facade is often achieved by a repetition of proportions. In a colonial facade, for example, small scale windows, large scale windows, and doorways will have similar proportions. Such redundancy or similarity might derive from a similarity of function of the windows, but it might also be a deliberate attempt to achieve the rest and calm that this unity of proportions provides. A heavy outline of the window may be most effective in identifying similarities of proportion. However, some people include diagonal lines to underscore the relationship be-

tween proportions. Such a drawing makes these relationships clearer and leaves an impression on the perception of the person doing the drawings that will carry over into other observations and design. Making this type of drawing also forces one to look carefully at various parts of a building and understand their sizes, proportions, and positions.

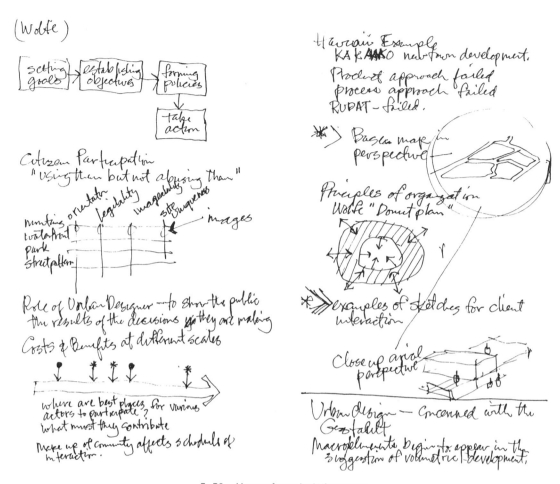

5-56 Uses of symbols in notes.

Symbols

In conventional writing there are visual marks or signals used to assist reading. For example, the separation between sets of sentences forming paragraphs is a way of signaling that the writer is moving from one idea to another. Indentation brings further emphasis to this change from one paragraph to the next. Other signals are used for added emphasis; one may underline words, print them in a heavier typeface, or repeat the words outside the body of the text. In visual notation, similar devices are available. To separate two ideas, a line may suffice. If the two ideas are separate but strongly related, a dashed or dotted line may convey that subtlety. For emphasis, there are a number of possibilities: circle the element which is the most important, draw an arrow pointing at the important idea, or use an asterisk to call attention. (Asterisks are sort of substitutes for stars.) A range of importance can be conveyed by using multiple arrows or other marks. Generally, symbols are a matter of personal choice, a personal code. Within this book you will find a variety of symbols or marks used for identification or emphasis. On these pages we present additional examples you may find useful.

5-57

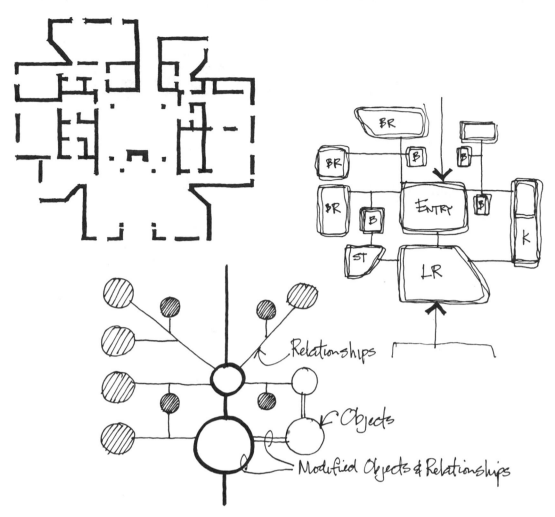

5-58 Degrees of abstraction, Goldenberg House by Louis Kahn.

Diagrams

A diagram is a simple, rapid method for representing the underlying structure or relationships in either a physical setting, physical design, or in the process by which something operates. Diagrams help make sense out of a complex whole and structure one's ideas. The most basic type is the bubble diagram, so named because it is a drawing consisting primarily of bubble-shaped objects connected by lines. The bubbles represent subjects or identities; the lines represent relationships or interactions between the subjects; both bubbles and lines are modified by the way in which they are drawn. To make effective use of bubble diagrams we need to adopt some rules, a visual grammar similar to the grammar that makes written language useful. Visual grammar provides organization or structure. Organization may be expressed through proximity that conveys which elements are closely related and which have more

tenuous relationships; direct linkage where a system of lines is used to indicate different types of relationships between parts; geometric order, positioning bubbles in a line or other configuration such as a square, triangle or circle; identity: related parts have common shapes, size, or color/value or are represented by a common symbol. Each of these ordering methods helps create a hierarchy of subjects (bubbles) and symbolizes other relationships. Both the bubbles and the lines can be modified through a number of techniques; thickening or doubling of lines or circles creates a hierarchy of importance while dashed or dotted lines convey subtler connections or items of lesser importance. On these pages we illustrate different types of identifying elements, relationships, and modifications to give you some idea of the range available.

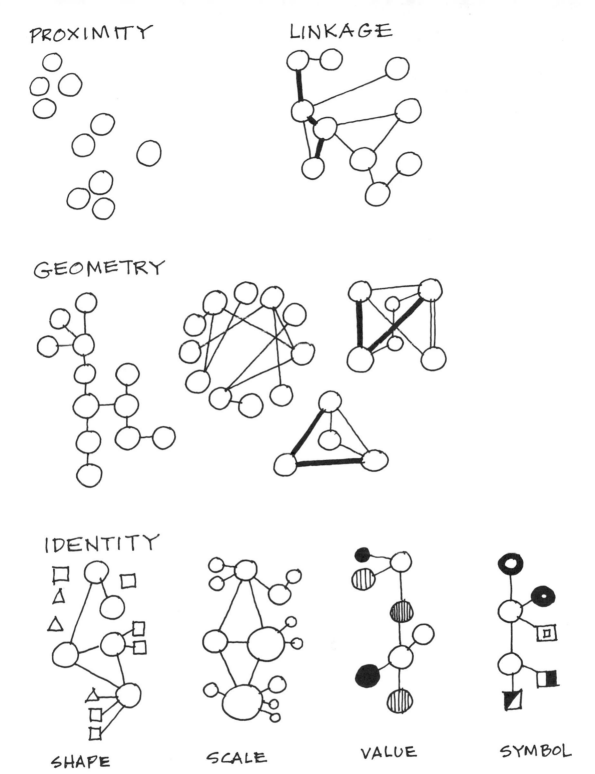

PROXIMITY

LINKAGE

GEOMETRY

IDENTITY

SHAPE

SCALE

VALUE

SYMBOL

5-59 Organizing systems for diagrams.

AREA DIAGRAMS

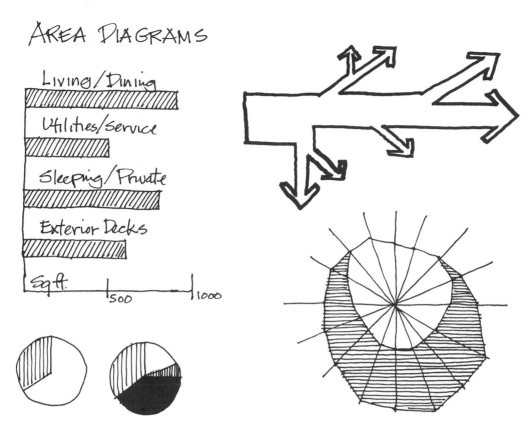

5-60 Area Diagrams.

Area Diagram/Matrix/Network

In addition to the bubble diagram we can identify three other major types of diagrams, namely, the area diagram, the matrix, and the network. The area diagram represents information by the size and configuration of zones that are identified. To take the most elementary example, a bar chart establishes relationships between factors by the size of the bars. A sun path diagram explains the daily cycle of the sun by the configuration of the shaded areas. The matrix diagram, on the other hand, is a coordinate system to identify relationships between identities. The matrix is like a filing cabinet in which you put ideas so that you can better retrieve them and profile the system you are describing. The network diagram is a linked linear model usually sequenced from left to right which can convey processes.

In our research for this book we found that no two notebooks are alike. Each person adopts conventions or a style of sketching which is most comfortable. The examples provided in this chapter are simply starting points. As you become more involved in keeping notes, you will depart from these examples and invent your own methods of notation. The people we interviewed enjoyed note-taking; they used it to meet their personal needs for expression or amusement. We encourage you to adapt from this chapter that which is most appropriate to your needs.

THE MATRIX

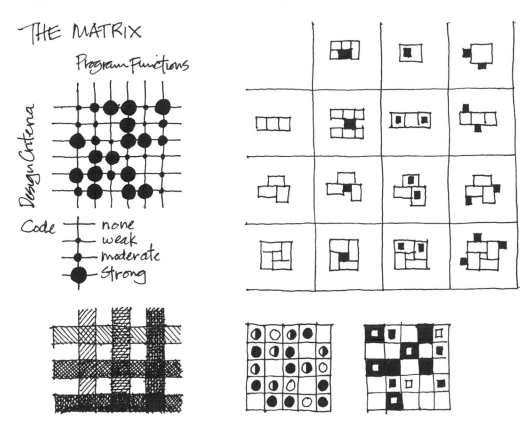

5-61 Matrices.

NETWORKS

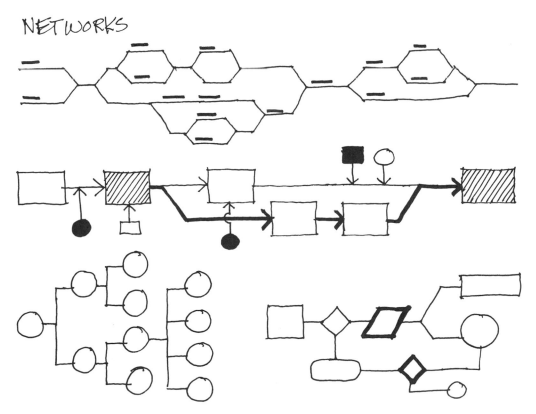

5-62 Networks.

Conclusion

6-1

In this book we first introduced the concept of a visual notebook and its contribution to visual literacy, followed by a description of the basic note-taking processes: recording, analysis, and design. Samples from a typical notebook journal illustrated the various opportunities for taking notes and their application to design. This was followed by notes from a number of different people within and outside the design professions, suggesting the broad potential of note-taking. Then the final chapter described equipment and methods with which to start taking notes.

In closing, we pause to say something about food. (Every book should have something to say about food.) A gourmet is described as one who has developed a refined taste for food and drink. Many people add measurably to the enjoyment of their lives by treating food as more than a necessity, as something that makes each day or portion of a day a special event, something which raises the quality of their lives. They raise their expectations about eating and therefore raise the quality of experience. In doing this, they seek variety not only in the way the food is cooked but in the way it is presented and in the environment that is the setting for eating.

Creative people often treat their work in a similar manner. They consider its setting, style, and content as occasions for enjoyment. They raise their expectations about the quality of their work and its contribution to their lives. For those whom we interviewed in preparing this book, sketching is a part of the quality of working and living; it is a source of pleasure. And over the years they have developed an aesthetic sensitivity to their drawings and the way they think which gives it a specific style or flavor. We would like to think that note-taking can play an important role in that pursuit.

Epilogue

Least we leave our readers with the notion that visual notes can stand on their own as a medium for capturing visual information, we have included this essay by the architect Thomas Beeby. Here the dialectic between a verbal and a visual world is complete. Neither could exist without the other. It is a dialectic between words which recount a segment of a "history" (in this case, largely fanciful) and visions which generate the tangible evidence of those imagined past events.

We offer Mr. Beeby's essay as a sort of epilogue, even though it does not sum-up the foregoing as an epilogue ought. It does, however, provide a rather lyrical ending for our discussion and may, we hope, offer an encouraging prospect for a medium which can be as lyrical as it is practical.

When asked to write an essay to accompany this book, my thoughts turned immediately to drawings I made for the "Seven Chicago Architects" show at the Richard Gray Gallery in Chicago. The process involved in conceiving and executing these drawings changed my entire outlook on architecture and opened my eyes to a world of symbolic imagery that has affected all of my buildings from that time to this day. This process of conceiving the drawings involved exploring their setting through a narrative of my own invention. Visual images were generated out of this narrative and quickly "caught" by visual notes before they could evaporate from memory's fickle grasp. Thus recorded, the images were ready to reflect the narrative and to be reflected back upon it in a dialectic between thought and vision.

Examining the catalog from that show in Chicago, I again read the statement that had accompanied my drawings:

"The house is built within the ruins of an abandoned Midwestern farm. The almost classical parts are reassembled into a sanctuary of civilization employing the imagery of Rome inherited from Palladio, Jefferson, and Adler. The forms of this tradition deal with pastoral themes leading to Arcady and beyond, to the gods and goddesses of the earth, water, air, and fire.

The language of classical architecture offers images pregnant with symbolic meaning. It is a visual and literary path to the subconscious fantasies of man, difficult to touch through the means of abstraction. The central half-domed pavilion rises from the ruins of the barn. It is a terrestrial being, vertical, centralized, compact. A central steel column passes on axis through the house; the half-dome is cut away to allow clear passage from heaven to earth. Steel loggias, ramps, and walkways extend to connect outbuildings. The entrance elevation is closed and formidable with a long ceremonial path past the relocated schoolhouse through an old cemetery gate, under an orchard and around an obelisk before arriving at the entry ramp. In contrast, the rear elevation is open to the garden, the heart of the house. At night, the central light guides visitors up the drive like a guardian eye and bathes the entire house and garden area with soft reflected light. Reception is at the level of the conservatory, which is flanked by two finch cages overlooking the garden. A steep, serpentine stair winds around the central column from the conservatory up to the platform of daydreams. Generous symmetrical stairs descend to the garden through the darkness of the grotto. Water drops around the dining area from the walls of the conservatory above. The for-

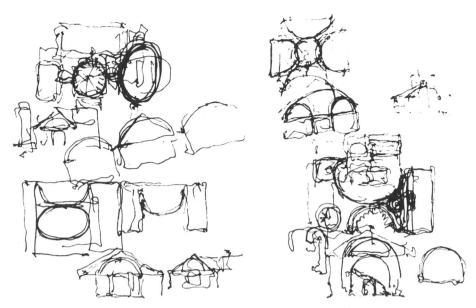

E-1　Visual notes by Thomas Beeby for a House of Virgil.

mal garden is defined by the stone walls of the old livestock enclosure. Water is channeled from the grotto throughout the garden, finally spilling over stone steps into the great pond, the mirror of heaven. In the ruin of the silo is the chamber of fire. The smoke rises through the opening at the top, forming the visible breath of the house. Facing the garden in the converted stable, each stall is an austere sleeping cell. The spring house is converted into a glass roofed bath with three pools offering hot, cold, or tempered water. The old farmhouse is the home of the caretaker, and although this is a working farm, it is built for the purposes of enchantment."

This statement, written at the time of the exhibition, only partially explained the true meaning of the drawings, for my most personal feelings had been severed from the text to permit a critical analysis of an objective nature. Attempting to reconstruct the exact process of creation, I searched further back into my mind for an explanation.

As an architect, I was trained to remember the great buildings of modern architecture but not to copy them. Historical style was presented in survey courses as a continuous stream of images that somehow supported the notion that only the aesthetics of Modernism were appropriate for our

age. Those apparitions that were supposedly only a preamble to reality, however, haunted my academic and early professional life, filling my dreams with an architecture that might be possible again. "The House of Virgil" project of 1976 was my first attempt to employ imagery from the past in a direct way.

I probed my mind for the most evocative visions that might come from personal recollections of meaningful memories. Searching my library for inspiration, I rediscovered old friends such as *The Sacred and Profane* by Mircea Eliade, *The Poetry of Space* by Gaston Bachelard, and *Architecture, Mysticism and Myth* by William Lethaby. At the library of the Illinois Institute of Technology (of all places) was a marvelous study of mythology called *Fairy Faith in Celtic Lands* by W. Y. Evans-Wentz. I also waded through the *Golden Bough* again.

Over the years, my interest in art had provided a stack of books that suddenly were perceived in a new way. Paintings from the American Luminist movement of the nineteenth century and the earlier German Romantic painters, Friedrich and Runge, spoke clearly to me from the past. Children's stories projected images of great clarity through illustrations by Dulac, Robinson, and even Maxfield Parrish. Isolated artists of personal vision—including

201

George de la Tour, Lorrain, and Flaxman—had always moved me, as had Nolde. I realized that all of these images were permanently hidden away somewhere in my mind, where they had been selected and stored for a decade or longer.

Palladio loomed as a major source of architectural iconography. Through my familiarity with the work of Mies van der Rohe, Schinkel emerged as a rival to Palladio in the power and originality of his vision. His predecessors, David and Friedrich Gilly, offered a stark and simplified vocabulary of power. The relationship between the architects and painters remained an intriguing puzzle.

I also found that my recollections from childhood provided a continuous stream of visual memories that I secretly treasured, particularly the American Midwestern landscape with its groupings of white frame structures, of such touching fragility, rising above the fields in never ending variations on a theme of vernacular building. Summers as a child had been spent exploring the wonders of a family farm with its pastures, woods, and streams. All this was indelibly printed on my mind but inaccessible as a result of my professional training.

Work on the drawings for the "House of Virgil" began slowly. My wife and I were spending all our free time in the country, restoring our newly acquired nineteenth-century schoolhouse. The building itself had become a symbol to us of the power of the past. Between labors, I would often lie on my back looking into the changing clouds, dreaming. Slowly a myth born from memory began to form in my mind, uniting the flood of images that flowed through it. By shutting my eyes as the hot summer sun beat down on my face, the sound of the wind in the grass slowly faded away and the story unfolded. This is that story.

There was a beautiful land located between the waters of the Great Inland Lakes and the Mighty River. It was called the Driftless Region, rising above the prairie like an island in a sea of grass. By some inexplicable quirk of history, the glaciers parted in their movement southward, creating a natural paradise, a literal Garden of Eden. Theory has it that the ancestry of all of Nature (for many days travel in any direction) owes its existence to the accident that spared this region from the death grip of the invading ice that ground the earth flat all around.

The mysterious island with its serpentine valleys, caves, and ominous rock formations lay for millenia under the control of Nature. In summer, the sun rose over the rolling grass and sent its beam shining onto the upturned faces of the flowers. Each morning, a new rose opened to the sun, the petals from those of the previous day falling to the earth. Swallows floated over the prairie gathering insects, in the evening dipping down to skim over the still waters of ponds, sending out circles of ripples as their wings touched their mirrored surface. Every year the endless chains of migrating birds passed overhead, and their voices were heard as they followed the sun on its eternal path.

The trees stood in groves, fighting to maintain a foothold against the hostile, invading grasses. Each year the prairie burned. The sky was darkened with smoke by day and illuminated by a brilliant orange by night. The sun was obscured for weeks as the advancing army of flames consumed everything in its path. Lightning unleashed by the mountainous clouds of summer sparked the dry grasses to start the inferno, and the ensuing rains did not always extinguish the storms' fiery progeny. The passing of the storms was signaled by the iridescent rings of the rainbows that arched from the still waters of the ponds up to their vaporous, celestial home.

The land was occupied by hunters, a race of people who were also great builders. They constructed vast complexes of raised earthen mounds in the form of their ancestors, whom they believed to be the animals and birds that shared their land. These hunters knew that they were part of Nature. When they mysteriously disappeared, the only evidence of their occupation were the monuments. Looking down from the heavens, the sculpted effigies of swallows glided over the ground, carrying with them the spirits of the departed.

New tribes of hunters then lived on the land as part of Nature; they built no lasting artifacts to celebrate their presence, for they were always drifting towards the setting sun, pushed on their way by hostile brothers escaping from the East. A new force was at work on the land, a new people of a different race were invading from across the Great Sea, destroying Nature's undisputed control of the land and bringing their own God with them.

The first appearance of these intruders marked a change in the perception of the cosmic order, for these men carried

E-2 Existing school house on the site, "a plane cubic volume" of the early settlers.

dreams of another sort than those of the hunters. The first of them came to rob the bounty of the land—furs to be sold in the corrupt land they came from and metal to make projectiles of death. Following them came farmers in search of Nature's treasure. Fearful of the immensity of the prairie, they huddled in the groves and ventured out by day to break a thousand years of unrestrained growth, exposing the virgin soil beneath. The organic treasure that had taken from the beginning of time to create was destroyed in a decade by their greed. The first settlers abandoned their temporary sod dens and moved further west in search of new land, following the traders and miners. The winds over the prairie began to carry the dust that would eventually darken the sky; the streams ran brown.

The next people came to stay. They came to farm the land but they also viewed it as their home. Memories of other places from their country beyond the Great Inland Lakes provided visions of domesticity. The Wilderness was demonic and had to be pushed beyond the edges of their domain. Order was imposed on Nature, the rocks cleared from the fields and laid up in enclosing walls to create a precinct for civilization amid the chaos. Gardens were planted to insure subsistence through the long winters when the cold winds blew off the prairie. Water was drawn from the springs that fed the ponds. Their first houses were plain cubic volumes, built of wood. Entirely unself-conscious in construction, they were identical in conception with the service buildings used for the shelter of animals. Modesty was a virtue, for the only reward in life lay beyond death and material gratification was forbidden. The land was appreciated but not loved. Sitting at the family table while reading the Book, the glow of the prairie fires at night signified the coming Holocaust of the Last Days when the rising sun would shine through a rosy sky on the Chosen. The mounds of the hunters were plowed under as a symbolic exorcism of the pagan spirits that possessed the land. For all that, the swallows still floated over the grass and skimmed the pond at dusk dipping, their wings into the still waters.

Generations passed, and the farmers prospered. Towns sprang up and the harshness of pioneer life waned. The God of the farmers came to be perceived as a more benign and less demanding presence. The prairie fires no longer burned; the only smoke rose from the chimneys of the houses, signifying the warmth of the hearth. Prosperity allowed new houses to replace ramshackled collections of rooms constructed over the years. Carpenters came from the new towns with plans of houses built across the Great Inland Lakes. To satisfy their desire for civilization, the wealthy farmers chose houses that would suggest a cultural credibility that exceeded their actual knowledge of both themselves and their society. Behind the facades of high architecture lay houses not dissimilar from the older houses that they replaced. The windows and doors, as well as the eaves, carried crude moldings of symbolic origin, often awkward and idiosyncratic. The plans suggested a symmetry found in a higher order of building from the past, while inside the detailing of stairs and mantles sufficed to indicate the farmers' aspirations. These houses represented a continuing effort by the invading peoples from the East to bring the vast power of the land under control by reconstructing it within the memory of their past. The architectural symbols they employed had a long history that went beyond the lands east of the Great Inland Lakes to the Old World where these same symbols had been protected from barbarism during the Dark Ages. Their origins lay in roots of great antiquity, from which they developed over the centuries, parallel-

ing similar achievements in art, philosophy, and literature. The power of the symbols was proven by their appearance at this outpost of civilization, in the hands of embattled farmers as a weapon against the overpowering force of Nature.

The first public buildings further illustrated the power of the symbolic elements to represent the aspirations of all the people. Practical building arrangement now was replaced by the symmetry that represented Antiquity. Architectural elements were detailed with entirely symbolic echoes of the past; regularity replaced random organization. With these public buildings, the farmers established a hold on the land and transformed it into a world subservient to their own culture. The prairie became meadow; the garden was filled with flowers from the Old World; Nature was replaced by Landscape. On lonely hilltops, fences were raised and gateways provided to bring the dead to a final resting place; lilies were placed each year on their graves. Nevertheless, the wild rose still grew on the borders of the graves. Each morning a new rose opened to the sun, the petals from the previous day falling to the earth. The color of the rose was now seen as being stained red by the blood of a martyred God who died at another time far away.

The ambition of the farm families drew them down the roads and into the towns where they became merchants. There they might enjoy more comforts and a more secure community. There they were also freed from working with their hands forever. The power and mystery of Nature no longer had a hold on them. The birds still migrated in pursuit of the sun, but their voices were no longer heard.

The discarded farms were bought by emigrant families from the Old World. They also brought their own set of dreams and languages with them. Memories of the ordered fields of their homeland recalled the pastoral equilibrium achieved through centuries of cultivation. As these emigrants roamed the fields of their new land, they saw familiar flowers with long folk traditions behind them and trees with magic powers, similar to those in the Old World. The very land itself spoke to them with familiar voices of myth and legend. Birds and animals again had a place in a mythic imagination that had evolved from centuries of working the land. Imaginary creatures from folk tradition also stirred in their minds. Unicorns might now be seen grazing in the meadows, bearing their vir-

gin riders. Spirits of the air, water, and earth escaped from the collective consciousness to inhabit the fields and groves.

The emigrants brought a new pattern of farming and a heightened vision of domestic order onto the land. The front enclosures, bound by stone walls, were straightened and completed to keep stray animals out. Orchards were planted in orderly grids and carefully manicured. Herds of cattle from the Old World grazed peacefully in fields girded by hedgerows. New stone barns were carefully raised stone by stone, as if growing out of the earth. Their forms followed the patterns evolved over centuries in the minds of these herdsmen. Stock enclosures and stables were built behind the barns, and spring houses to keep milk fresh even in the hot, silent days of summer. Cows gathered in the water of the ponds to cool off as they patiently awaited the hour of milking. The groves were meticulously carved into woodlots and harvested for firewood. Patiently these emigrants shaped the land into an image of pastoral order that might match their dimming memory of the Old World.

They inhabited houses as they received them, for the symbolic language spoke to them as it had to their builders. The herdsmen filled these houses with treasures from other places. Some of their possessions spoke the same language as the houses but with an overlay of the even older language of myth, which coexisted with the symbols borrowed from the Antique. For over a century, the dreams of both herdsmen and farmers had been absorbed into a composite image that was now common over the entire region.

Once again, however, people left the land for life in the towns and cities, and the evolution of the social order now worked to destroy their vision of the land. Changing patterns of inheritance and farming practices forced an abandonment of the old-style family farm. The dreams of generations were helpless to stave off the economic realities dictated by mechanization. Once prosperous farms lay in splendid disuse in the valleys; machines came and leveled in one day what took a century to create.

Some of the workers in the cities and towns now came to feel the exile of being separated from the land and its regenerating mythic force. They returned to the valleys and saw the abandoned farms, untended by the love of inhabitation, surrendering to the ubiquitous grass that in-

E-3 Interior of the school house after the architect and his family's third year there.

vaded the enclosing walls and swirled around the limestone foundations. The cubic volumes, in their disrepair, especially touched the hearts of these visitors because symbolism in their day become forbidden in building. On a hot summer day, the sunshine reflected from the aged whitewashed surfaces was still almost blinding in its purity. Fugitive day lilies, phlox, and hollyhocks were reminders of earlier gardens—traces of a flowered paradise. Wild roses and hawthorns, impervious to a century of grazing by virtue of their armament of thorns, reclaimed the once-manicured fields. Clematis vines still clung tenaciously to the turned posts of the porches, tendrils worming their way beneath the checkered layers of paint into the cracks and fissures of the aged wood. Tears filled the eyes of the returning fugitives from the cities as they realized the loss they had suffered by sacrificing their past.

One of these intruders was an architect. He stood with his family in the abandoned farm yards. The song of the insects in the plants and of the birds overhead rose above the constant whisper of the wind as it moved through the grasses around the empty buildings. They looked at the ruins of what was (as once the inhabitants must have) with sympathy and concern. They saw ants moving in long lines over stone

foundations on their way to work in the dark recesses of the structure, hastening the day when man's dreams for the land come to an end and Nature returns to conquer. Through broken windows, hornets invaded the coolness of shaded interiors, sharing the dark rooms with a myriad of night-flying creatures that sought concealment from the sun in the crevices of broken walls. Swallows fearlessly darted through unhinged doors to find their young. Throughout the labyrinth within the walls, the mice ran silently, making nests from the discarded refuse of forgotten families. Hiding in the stone cave formed by the foundation walls, the predators of night slept. In the dampness, the vapors rising up from the earth threatened the ancient wood members that had once been protected from the ravages of their enemy, water.

The stone barn walls stood precariously near the ruins of the silos. The few blackened remains of monumental wood structures attested to a great fire long ago. The horror of a barn fire, its flames illuminating the dark night and surrounding fields, is not easily forgotten. Like a great ship burning at sea, its inferno was reflected in the mirror of the ponds beyond. Promise of a rich harvest had been reversed by a consuming catastrophe that drove the last inhabitants off the land. Loading their belongings into trucks, they departed, never to return. The grass advanced and removed all traces of the access roads, leaving only ruins as a poignant reminder of man's abandonment of the land.

The architect and his family searched for a building that might return them to the past. They found a remote, devastated school house on one acre of precious soil. It had the meaning to them (as it had had to its builders) of a communal pride of place and the power of symbolic architecture. Lovingly, they spent a year cleaning out the ravaged interior. A second year passed as they restored the fabric of its interior. Before the job was finished, a third year had passed. During this time they watched the planets rise and set, the swallows float over the grass, and the rose open each day. They collected the abandoned treasures of the farmers and herdsmen and furnished the house with them. As they walked the fields, they found the lost implements of the hunters who first inhabited the valleys. They stood on the mounds and looked over the land, feeling the power of the past to impart meaning to the present. The fields and groves still held the mythic spirits brought to the land by its inhabitants.

The architect looked closely at his building and its symbolic details. They spoke of aspirations to turn Wilderness into Civilization. The entire structure spoke to him of man's desire to create an ordered cosmic vision through the use of symbols of the past, a vision both idealistic and humane despite overwhelming evidence that it is not a true representation of historical reality. This vision allowed for, and was even based on, the mythic traditions of the land, permitting personal interpretation without losing its ability to communicate a message of the power of cultural memory.

At the end of a hard day of labor on his land, the architect's thoughts drifted into a dream-vision that attempted somehow to gather all his memories together in one building, a sanctuary for everything that he held dear. For an entire summer, he allowed his mind to wonder freely, ransacking his memory in search of images that would best express the emotions he felt toward architecture and his world. He was deeply troubled by his apparent inability to probe his memory for visions of potency. He found that the images seemed to come from three sources. First, there were images of a universal nature that appeared to be drawn from the unconscious and were characterized by the kind of iconography found in fairy tales, mythology, and dreams. A second series of images was retrieved from his cultural memory that dealt with the shared meanings of his civilization, including the symbolic elements of architecture. Finally, personal recall provided a rich world of evocative memories that had helped shape his development as an individual. He felt it must be possible for an architectural iconography to display profound resonance at all three of these levels of comprehension. He came to realize that there is a mechanism that can make this possible. It is the phenomenon that occurs when personal memory withdraws from everyday life to the shadowed recesses of the solitary mind and merges into the universal world of the dream. The cycle of memory retreats from the conscious world of shared reality through the personal domain of individual recollection into the potent world of myth and dream to form symbolic images that are strained through the three levels of memory and can be appreciated finally on a conscious level. As he followed this path through the mind, images appeared that moved him greatly. Slowly a narrative developed that ordered these images into a story and allowed him to transmute them into drawings.

This is that narrative; without it, the drawings would have been impossible to conceive. Without the drawings, the buildings that followed would have been impossible to realize. Dream and reality have become one again.

Thomas H. Beeby

Close your physical eye, so that you first see your picture with your spiritual eye. Then bring to light what you have seen in the dark so that it is passed on to others from the outside to the inside.

C. G. Friedrich

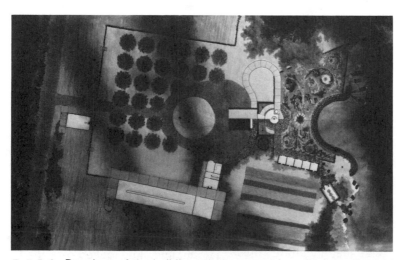

E-4, 5, 6 Drawings of the buildings that emerged from the narrative and the image of a House of Virgil.

E-5

E-6

Footnotes

1. Dondis, D. A. *A Primer of Visual Liter acy*. Cambridge, MA: MIT Press, 1973, pp. 67–81.
2. Dondis, *A Primer of Visual Literacy*, p. 74.
3. Edwards, Betty. *Drawing on the Right Side of the Brain*. Los Angeles: J.P. Tarcher, Inc., 1979, pp. 25–43.
4. Adams, James L. *Conceptual Block-busting*. New York: Scribner, 1974.
5. Pye, David. *The Nature of Design*. New York: Reinhold Publishing Corporation, 1964.
6. Piet Hein has made many bridges be-tween art and science often with spec-tacular results. In addition to his "super egg" he invented the Soma Cube as a result of his attempts to ex-plain quantum theory.
7. Fischer, Edward. "The Recorded Life". *Notre Dame Magazine*. Notre Dame, IN: University of Notre Dame, December 1981. p. 17–21.
8. As quoted in the forward to Auden, W.H. *A Certain World.* New York: The Viking Press, 1970.
9. Norberg-Schulz, Christian. *Genius Loci*. New York: Rizzoli International, 1980.
10. See the bibliography for references to books by Arnheim.
11. Edwards, *Drawing on the Right Side of the Brain,* p. 40.
12. Edwards, *Drawing on the Right Side of the Brain,* pp. 5–6.
13. Edwards, *Drawing on the Right Side of the Brain*, p. 192.
14. From an article by Michael Graves. "The Necessity for Drawing: Tangible Speculation." *Architectural Design 6/77.* New York: Vol. 47, No. 6, pp. 384–394, 1977.

Illustration and Photo Credits:

Bibliography

VISUAL AND DRAWING THEORY:

Arnheim, Rudolf. *The Dynamics of Architectural Form*. Berkeley, CA: University of California Press, 1977.

Arnheim, Rudolf. *Art and Visual Perception: The New Vision*. Berkeley, CA: University of California Press, 1974.

Arnheim, Rudolf. *Visual Thinking*. Berkeley. CA: University of California Press, 1969.

Dondis, D.A. *A Primer of Visual Literacy*. Cambridge, MA: The MIT Press, 1973.

Edwards, Betty. *Drawing on the Right Side of the Brain*. Los Angeles: J.P. Tarcher, Inc., 1979

Gombrich, E.H. *The Sense of Order*. Ithaca, NY: Cornell University Press, 1979.

Huxley, A. *The Art of Seeing*. Seattle: Madrona Publishers, 1975.

Pye, David. *The Nature of Design*. New York: Reinhold Publishing Corporation, 1964.

Sommer, Robert. *The Mind's Eye.* New York: Dell Publishing, 1978.

Wechsler, Judith (Ed.). *On Aesthetics in Science*. Cambridge, MA: The MIT Press, 1978.

NOTEBOOKS AND NOTATION:

Architectural Sketches & Flower Drawings by Charles Rennie Mackintosh. New York: Rizzoli Publications, Inc., 1977.

Bucher, Francois. *Architector: The Lodge Books and Sketch Books of Medieval Architects*. Vols. 1 & 2. New York: Abaris Books, 1979.

DaVinci, Leonardo. *Notebooks*. New York: Dover Publications, Inc., 1970.

Feldman, Eugene and Wurman, Richard Saul *The Notebooks and Drawings of Louis I. Kahn*. Philadelphia: Falcon Press, 1962, distributed by Wittenborn and Company.

Hogarth, Paul and Spender, Stephen. *America Observed*. New York: Clarkson N. Potter, Inc., 1979.

Le Corbusier Selected Drawings. introduction by Michael Graves, New York: Rizzoli International Publications, 1981.

Le Corbusier Sketchbooks. Vols. 1–4. Cambridge, MA: The Architectural History Foundation and The MIT Press, 1981–82.

The Notebook of Paul Klee. Vol. 1: The Thinking Eye. New York: Wittenborn, 1978.

Steinberg, Saul. *The Passport*. New York: Random House, Inc., 1979.

DRAWING AND GRAPHICS:

Ching, Frank. *Architectural Graphics*. New York: Van Nostrand Reinhold Company, 1975.

Czaja, Michael. *Freehand Drawing: Language of Design*. Walnut Creek, CA: Gambol Press, 1975.

Edwards, Betty. *Drawing on the Right Side of the Brain*. Los Angeles: J.P. Tarcher, Inc., 1979

Hanks, Kurt and Belliston, Larry. *Draw! A Visual Approach to Thinking, Learning, and Communicating*. Los Altos, CA: William Kaufmann, Inc., 1977.

Hogarth, Paul. *Drawing Architecture*. New York: Watson-Guptill Publications, Inc., 1973.

Lockard, William Kirby. *Design Drawing*. Revised Edition. Tucson, AZ: Pepper Publishing, 1982.

McGinty, Tim. *Drawing Skills in Architecture*. Dubuque, Iowa: Kendall/Hunt Publishing Co., 1976.

McKim, Robert H. *Experiences in Visual Thinking*. Monterey, CA: Brooks/Cole, 1972.

Thiel, Phillip. *Freehand Drawing, A Primer.* Seattle: University of Washington Press, 1965.

Index